Praise for *Give My Swiss Chards to Broadway*

"As arguably one of the world's worst cooks, this delightfully punny
ode to food and Broadway inspired me to pick back up my oven mitts and
try my hand at some Weenie Todds. Thank you to Adam and Gideon,
and sorry to my friends and family."

RACHEL BROSNAHAN

"Cooking gives me stage fright. But by combining my great ineptitude
(cooking) with my great passion (theater), Gideon and Adam have created
the perfect vehicle for me—and any other theater queen with cooking
jitters—to rise above the performance anxiety and deliver the goods."

JONATHAN GROFF

"What a truly original and innovative way into an incredibly fun
cookbook. As someone who is not always adept in the kitchen, marrying
cooking and musical theater makes me want to bust out my whisk,
get adventurous, and belt out some showtunes while cooking!"

ANDREW RANNELLS

GIVE MY SWISS CHARDS TO BROADWAY

GIVE MY SWISS CHARDS TO BROADWAY

The BROADWAY LOVER'S COOKBOOK

GIDEON GLICK *and* ADAM ROBERTS

ILLUSTRATED BY JUSTIN "*Squigs*" ROBERTSON

For information about permission to reproduce selections from this book, write to
Permissions, Countryman Press, 500 Fifth Avenue, New York, NY 10110

For information about special discounts for bulk purchases, please contact
W. W. Norton Special Sales at specialsales@wwnorton.com or 800-233-4830

Manufacturing by Versa Press
Book design by Raphael Geroni
Production manager: Devon Zahn

Countryman Press
www.countrymanpress.com

An imprint of W. W. Norton & Company, Inc.
500 Fifth Avenue, New York, NY 10110
www.wwnorton.com

978-1-68268-718-5

10 9 8 7 6 5 4 3 2 1

From Gideon:

To Perry, who scarfed down more puns and
recipes than he bargained for; and to my family,
who aided and abetted my sick passion for theater.

From Adam:

To my parents, who taught me to love food
and musicals; and to Craig, who's as enthusiastic
about my cooking as he is annoyed by the show
tunes that I blast in the kitchen.

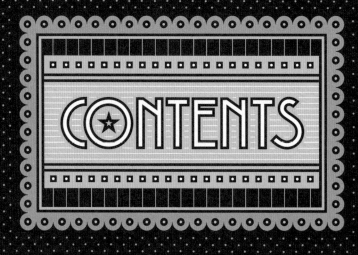

Overture

WELCOME TO *GIVE MY SWISS CHARDS TO BROADWAY*, A COOKBOOK written for musical theater fans who love to cook and vice versa. In these pages, you'll find our culinary tributes to the Great White Way, with everything from breakfasts (The Muesli Man, page 18) to appetizers (Weenie Todds, page 48) to soups and salads (Little Chop of Horrors, page 79) to entrées (Sunday in the Pork with George, page 124) to desserts (Wickedoodles, page 168).

When we set out to write this book, we wanted to combine some of our favorite things: our love for musical theater, our love for puns, our love for cooking, and obviously, raindrops on roses and whiskers on kittens. One of us (Adam) is a food writer who's obsessed with Broadway musicals; one of us (Gideon) is a Broadway musical actor who loves to eat. As fans of each other's work, the two of us became friends and cracked each other up during the pandemic, pitching musical theater recipe puns. We hope they crack you up, too, and inspire you to cook.

So saddle up that Bronco as you giddy-up to our Yolklahoma! (page 28). Get your hanky ready as Tony meets the same fate as the poultry in our Chicken Breast Side Story (page 112). And cue up that Jerry Herman classic as you pop the champagne and get your mold ready to make our Jell-O, Dolly! (page 162).

Along the way, you'll learn about some of Broadway's best tunes and all kinds of trivia about the shows that inspired these dishes. Did you know that when *Sunday in the Park with George* first premiered, it was only one act? Or that *Falsettos* was two separate shows? Or that parts of *Cabaret* were written at a dinner party? . . . Well now you do.

Most important, you'll learn all kinds of culinary tricks that'll ensure rave reviews from the harshest critics in your house.

So the next time you're sitting at home wondering what to make for dinner, cue up your favorite musical and make the dish that goes along with it. We guarantee there won't be empty chairs at empty tables for long, so be our guest, it's almost suppertime, why don't you stay for the night, or maybe a bite—

Sorry we got carried away. Let's get cooking!

Dance Ten, Cooks Three

Ten Tips for Getting Standing Ovations with Every Meal

· · · · · · · · ·

HAVE CONFIDENCE. Even Fräulein Maria had to pep herself up before becoming a governess, and it's no different in the kitchen. Take a few deep breaths and tell yourself, "I can do this" before tackling a recipe. Just make sure there's not a pine cone on your chair when you sit down for dinner.

LOOK BEFORE YOU LEAP. You can take us or leave us with this advice, but in our experience, it's always best to read the entire recipe through before making it.

BIT BY BIT, PUT IT TOGETHER. It might be tempting to jump right in and start cooking, but you'll do yourself a big favor if you chop the vegetables, measure the oils, and get everything ready to go before you start.

THE SUN'S A BALL OF BUTTER . . . SO USE IT! To be a good cook, you can't be afraid of fat or salt. Be generous with the fat (butter, olive oil) and salt the first time you make something and then, the next time you make it, cut back if you'd like (but why would you do that?).

PICK A LITTLE, TASTE A LITTLE. No recipe can tell you *exactly* how much salt or pepper or lemon juice or olive oil to add to it: you've got to trust your instincts. For example, every soup will be different based on how large the carrots are, how big the pot is, and whether the stock you use is already salted. The only way to ensure flavorful results is to taste and season as you go.

TAKE TIME TO LEARN, TIME TO CARE. If you're in a rush, make something you already know how to make. For new recipes, think of it as a leisurely activity on a weekend afternoon . . . if you enjoy yourself doing it, the food will taste better.

MIX IT IN A MIXER AND PRETEND IT'S BEEF. If you're a vegetarian, or don't eat red meat, don't let that stop you from making the recipes in this book. Feel free to substitute with Impossible Meat, ground chicken, turkey, etc. (Although kidney of a horse and liver of a cat are not recommended.)

'TIL YOU TRY, YOU'LL NEVER KNOW. If you're unsure of an ingredient or a technique—Urfa biber (a Turkish chili), charring a red pepper directly on the stove top—give it a go and see what you think. It's the only way to defy the gravity of your usual repertoire.

HAVE THE WHOLE WORLD ON A PLATE. If these recipes seem to make too much food, don't be afraid: it's always better to have too much at a dinner party than too little. And whatever is left over, you can eat for lunch the next day.

WE'RE GONNA GO THROUGH IT TOGETHER. You know what's more fun than writing a cookbook with a friend? Actually cooking with a friend. Open up your kitchen and share the stage with someone you love—unless they hog the spotlight, in which case, kick them out.

Sing Out, Swiss Cheese!

A Beginner's Guide to Listening to Musical Theater

. . . .

WHAT'S THE BEST WAY TO LISTEN TO A MUSICAL YOU DON'T know? This is a very good question that has haunted people for ages, or at least since . . . the gramophone? We don't have time to look that up. We're writing a cookbook here!

Where to start?

Well, first, it's important to know what goes into the musical you're listening to. What are the *ingredients*?

There is a composer who writes the music and a lyricist who writes the (you guessed it!) lyrics to the songs. Sometimes they're the same person, like a Stephen Sondheim or a Jason Robert Brown. Very erudite, very fancy pants.

There's also a book writer who writes the scenes and text between the songs and helps shape the story. Sometimes that happens to be the lyricist or composer, too. Also very erudite, very fancy pants.

Then you have your director, the person who stages and puts the show together, the choreographer who creates the dance numbers, and the music director (an *unsung* hero) who makes sure all the music components are working properly. Then obviously you have your cast who sings the whole darn thing.

Now before you listen . . .

It's VERY important to have some context for the show. When was it written? What was going on during that time? For example, *The Phantom of the Opera* came to Broadway in 1988 and people at that time were obsessed with chandeliers. (We can't actually fact-check that, but the '80s were all about opulence!) What we're trying to say is that having context for the show will deeply enrich your experience of the musical.

It's also very important to know what the show is about, as it's much more fun and fulfilling to listen to songs when you understand where they fit within the narrative and its themes. This isn't a regular album, this is a CAST album, people! A lot happens between songs and it's best not to get lost; otherwise the songs will lose their impact. Except for *Cats*. Don't worry about the plot for *Cats*.

You can listen to the songs first and go along for the ride, or look up the lyrics before or while you listen to the show, although that could be confusing if you're cooking at the same time, especially if you're looking up lyrics to *Sweeney Todd* (yikes!).

And lastly, make sure to turn up the volume—otherwise you won't hear anything.

Okay . . . you're ready to start consuming these musicals. And don't be nervous. You'll be swell, you'll be great, you'll have the whole world on a plate. Literally.

The Muesli Man

76 Rolled Oats Led the Nut Parade

• • •

Inspired by THE MUSIC MAN

Book, Music, and Lyrics by Meredith Willson

Opened on Broadway in 1957 at the Majestic Theatre

THERE WERE BELLS ON A HILL, BUT I NEVER HEARD THEM SINGING 'til there was . . . muesli. Before TV had Walter White and Tony Soprano, Broadway had Harold Hill. In *The Music Man*, Hill is a charming con man purporting to be a bandleader who convinces the denizens of River City, Iowa, to buy a plethora of instruments, which he promises to teach them to play. Secretly, though, Hill plans on skipping town before doing so, because as we remind you, he is a con man . . . with no discernible music skills. But, alas, a wise librarian, Marian (ugh, love a good rhyme) wises up to Hill and a love story unfolds! And this muesli will be a love story in your mouth. There's a Wells Fargo wagon–worth of ingredients, including raisins from Fresno and a box of maple sugar on my birthday (except you can get your raisins from anywhere, we're using maple syrup instead of maple sugar, and, importantly, it's not our birthday). We recommend singing "Goodnight, My Someone" to your muesli as you leave it overnight in the fridge to set up. Upon waking, you'll be hearing those bells on a hill as soon as you take your first bite.

2 cups rolled oats

¼ cup roughly chopped whole almonds

¼ cup shelled green pistachios

½ cup unsweetened coconut flakes

½ teaspoon salt

1 cup Greek yogurt

2 cups milk or milk substitute (oat would work great)

Zest from 1 orange

2 tablespoons maple syrup, plus more for drizzling

1 teaspoon vanilla

½ teaspoon cinnamon

¼ cup golden raisins

¼ cup chopped dried figs

1. Preheat the oven to 350°F.

2. On a baking sheet, toss together the rolled oats, almonds, pistachios, and coconut flakes with the salt. Spread out evenly and toast in the oven, stirring every 2 minutes, until everything is fragrant and the coconut is lightly golden brown, about 8 minutes. Set aside to cool.

3. In a separate bowl, whisk together the yogurt, milk, orange zest, maple syrup, vanilla, and cinnamon. Fold in the cooled toasted oats and nuts, plus the raisins and dried figs. Cover with plastic wrap and refrigerate overnight.

4. The next morning, stir well and serve in bowls with a drizzle of maple syrup.

RECIPE CONTINUES

Muesli, in and of itself, is just the dry stuff. What we have here is more like overnight oats, which marries all of the flavors beautifully. But if you're feeling Iowa stubborn, just omit the liquids and mix the toasted oats and nuts with the dried fruit and use them however you wish. For example, sprinkle it over a grapefruit from Tampa.

 Feel free to recast any of the nuts and dried fruits in this recipe (after all, Shirley Jones took the Barbara Cook part in the movie). Some great alternatives: pecans, walnuts, and hazelnuts for the nuts, and dried cranberries, apricots, and dates for the fruit.

 Did you know that the 1957 cast album for *The Music Man* was the first to ever receive a Grammy Award for Best Musical Theater Album? And you thought *Hamilton* was groundbreaking!

 The 1957 cast album also lasted 245 weeks on the Billboard charts, if that's any indication of how good its tunes are. Some favorites are "Seventy-Six Trombones," "Ya Got Trouble," "The Wells Fargo Wagon," and "'Til There Was You," which the Beatles actually covered. How groovy is that?

 One of the authors of this book (can you guess who?) played Winthrop in his fourth-grade school production, and he didn't even have to pretend to have a lisp. That came naturally.

The Book of Mormalade

Granny "Joseph" Smith Apple Jam on All-American Biscuits

• • •

Inspired by THE BOOK OF MORMON (THE MUSICAL)

Book, Music, and Lyrics by Trey Parker, Matt Stone, *and* Robert Lopez

Opened on Broadway in 2011 at the Eugene O'Neill Theater

HELLO, OUR NAMES ARE GIDEON AND ADAM, AND WE WOULD like to share with you the most amazing apple jam on a biscuit. From the creators of *South Park* (Trey Parker and Matt Stone), *The Book of Mormon* follows Elder Price and Elder Cunningham on a mission in Africa as they help spread the word of Mormonism. Along the way, Elder Cunningham starts spreading the word of not only Joseph Smith, but also Yoda, Darth Vader, hobbits, and Lt. Uhura from *Star Trek,* and Elder Price . . . gets the actual book of Mormon shoved up his bum (hasa diga eebowai, indeed). If only Elder Price had approached those warlords with these hot, buttery biscuits and homemade apple jam, he'd be in much better shape. If there's a voice in your head saying "I can't make homemade jam," turn it off. You can make the jam way ahead—it's just a matter of standing and stirring and watching—and this drop biscuit recipe, which is adapted from *Cook's Illustrated*, is so easy and satisfying, it'll have you singing "I Believe" the moment you see them puffing up in the oven. Even better than a trip to Sal Tlay Ka Siti.

RECIPE CONTINUES

FOR THE JAM

5 assorted apples (Granny Smith, Pink Lady, Honeycrisp, etc.), peeled, cored, and cut into ¾- to 1-inch pieces

1 cup water

½ cup granulated sugar

Zest and juice from 1 lemon

1 teaspoon cinnamon

½ teaspoon freshly ground nutmeg

½ teaspoon kosher salt

FOR THE BISCUITS

2 cups all-purpose flour, plus more for biscuit-shaping

1 tablespoon baking powder

1 tablespoon granulated sugar

1 teaspoon salt

½ teaspoon baking soda

4 tablespoons cold unsalted butter, plus 1 tablespoon melted

1½ cups cold buttermilk

TO MAKE THE JAM

1. Combine apples with the water in a saucepan and bring to a simmer. Cook for about 15 minutes, until the fruit is tender and the liquid is reduced.

2. Add the sugar, lemon zest and juice, cinnamon, nutmeg, and salt; stir and continue cooking at a moderate simmer until the mixture is thick, about 25 minutes more. You'll know it's done when you swipe a wooden spoon across the bottom of the pan and it leaves a path.

3. Ladle the hot mixture into a bowl or jar and allow to cool before using. It will keep for up to a week in the refrigerator, covered.

1. Preheat the oven to 500°F.

2. Spray a 9-inch cake pan with cooking spray.

3. Whisk together the flour, baking powder, sugar, salt, and baking soda. Cut the cold butter into cubes and toss with the flour mixture. Using two knives, a pastry cutter, or your own fingertips, work the butter into the flour, until the mixture looks like wet sand and there are pea-size chunks. With a rubber spatula, stir in the cold buttermilk.

4. In another bowl, pour in about a cup of flour. Spray a ¼-cup-capacity ice cream scoop or a ¼-cup measuring cup with cooking spray and scoop out ¼ cup of the wet dough and drop into the bowl with flour. Gently roll around in the flour and then lift into the prepared cake pan. Place the biscuits in a circle around the perimeter of the cake pan with the final biscuits inside. Brush the tops with the melted butter.

5. Bake for 5 minutes, then lower the oven temperature to 450°F and cook 15 minutes more. Allow to cool for a minute before turning out onto a plate. Eat with more butter slathered on, plus the apple jam.

COOKING NOTES

 Want a better way to peel apples? I swear I'm not making things up again, Arnold. Just slice the tops and bottoms off, then all you have to do is peel straight down. Goes much faster.

 Besides baptizing yourself with the apple jam, here are some other uses for it: Put it on top of waffles, eat it with vanilla ice cream, or you can use it with savory dishes like roast chicken or pork chops.

LISTENING NOTES

 Most shows take some time to develop themselves out of town, but the producers for this hit were so confident in its hit-ness that they decided to skip the out-of-town tryout and open right on Broadway. We'd say that paid off and so would their accountants.

 You might recognize the music of Robert Lopez from another Broadway musical, *Avenue Q*, but you probably know him better for his work on a tiny independent film called *Frozen*. Who says you can't work for *South Park* and Disney?

 Book of Mormon's book is quite lauded, but the tunes are excellent, too, which attests to the show's mega-hit status. "I Believe," "Hello!," and "Turn It Off" are real showstoppers.

Griddler on the Roof

Rich Man Challah French Toast with a Blueberry Blessing on Its Head

• • •

Inspired by FIDDLER ON THE ROOF

Music by Jerry Bock, *Lyrics by* Sheldon Harnick, *Book by* Joseph Stein

Opened on Broadway in 1964 at the Imperial Theatre

TO LIFE, TO LIFE, L'CHALLAH! BASED ON SHOLEM ALEICHEM'S *Tevye the Dairyman* and other short stories, first published in Yiddish in 1894, *Fiddler on the Roof* tells the tale of Tevye the milkman and his family in Russia. And let's just say, Tevye's got troubles. Right here in Anatevka (whoops, wrong show). Tevye has five, count 'em, five daughters, and his oldest three want to marry for love (can you believe it?). And if that's not troublesome enough, Jewish communities in Russia are being torn apart by pogroms. Ultimately, Tevye and his family are given three days to leave Anatevka for America, while a fiddler doesn't even help them pack, he just fiddles on the roof. And we believe it's best to never leave your homeland on an empty stomach, so let us suggest this French toast. Made with challah, three eggs, plus an egg yolk and lots of butter, it's very rich indeed. Sprinkled with a little confectioners' sugar, and anointed with a blueberry blessing on its head, this French toast isn't just breakfast—it's a miracle of miracles.

FOR THE BLUEBERRY BLESSING

1 cup fresh blueberries
¼ cup honey
Zest and juice from 1 large orange (about ¼ cup juice)
Kosher salt

FOR THE FRENCH TOAST

One 24-ounce loaf challah (unsliced)
2 cups whole milk
3 eggs plus 1 egg yolk
1 tablespoon honey
½ teaspoon cinnamon

½ teaspoon vanilla
Kosher salt
4 tablespoons butter
Confectioners' sugar

TO MAKE THE BLUEBERRY BLESSING

1. Preheat the oven to 250°F.

2. Make the blueberry blessing first by combining the blueberries, ¼ cup honey, the orange zest and juice, and a pinch of kosher salt in a small skillet. Turn up the heat to medium-high and cook, stirring occasionally with a heatproof rubber spatula, until the blueberries burst open and the mixture is juicy and thickened, 3 to 5 minutes. Set aside.

RECIPE CONTINUES

1. Using a serrated knife, slice your challah on the diagonal into one-inch slices. You should be able to get 8 slices total, not counting the butt ends.

2. In a large bowl or baking dish (easier for dipping), whisk together the milk, eggs, the tablespoon of honey, cinnamon, vanilla, and another pinch of kosher salt.

3. In a large nonstick or cast-iron skillet, melt two tablespoons of the butter on medium-high heat and swirl it all around so it coats the bottom. Dip the challah into the milk/egg mixture, making sure to soak it on both sides, but not so much that it falls apart. Allow excess to drip off and place in the hot butter. Repeat with two more slices, but don't crowd the skillet (you'll have to do this in batches).

4. Fry the French toast on one side until golden brown, 3 to 5 minutes, then flip and fry on the second side for another 2 to 3 minutes. Place the golden brown French toast pieces on a baking sheet and keep warm in the oven. Add another tablespoon of butter to the skillet and continue with the remaining challah slices and French toast batter, keeping the finished French toast warm in the oven on a baking sheet until all the pieces are finished.

5. To serve, use a sifter to dust the pieces with confectioners' sugar and serve with the blueberry blessing drizzled generously on top.

If you're making this at sunrise but want to pretend it's sunset (aka cocktail hour), you can add a little booze to the batter. Try adding a tablespoon of whiskey, cointreau, or dark rum and don't tell Yenta.

 It's a shanda if you can't find challah, but other breads will work with this recipe: brioche, sourdough, even plain old sandwich bread. But it's still best if you buy the loaf whole and slice thick slices yourself; otherwise the French toast will be too thin. Also, it's okay to buy the bread a day or two ahead. Staler is a better match for French toast.

LISTENING NOTES

 Did you know that Bette Midler made her Broadway debut in *Fiddler on the Roof*? She joined the original cast early in the run as Rivka and then took over the part of Tzeitel. That broom work in "Matchmaker" was clearly early training for Bette's portrayal of Winifred in Disney's *Hocus Pocus.* An auspicious start for our Jewish diva.

 In 2018, a production of *Fiddler on the Roof* was mounted Off-Broadway and performed completely in Yiddish. It opened to rave reviews and transferred to a commercial Off-Broadway run. It was directed by Joel Grey, the original Emcee. From the Weimar Republic to the shtetls of Russia. We stan!

 Tevye's showstopping act one number, "If I Were a Rich Man," was covered in a 2004 pop song called "Rich Girl." Can you guess by who? None other than Eve and Gwen Stefani, naturally. If only Tevye knew his thoughts would one day be a global pop hit, he wouldn't have had to worry about money at all, ya ha deedle deedle, bubba bubba deedle deedle dum.

Yolklahoma!

Fried Eggs on Farmer and the Cowhand Potatoes

• • •

Inspired by OKLAHOMA!

Music by Richard Rodgers, *Book and Lyrics by* Oscar Hammerstein II

Opened on Broadway in 1943 at the St. James Theatre

T HERE'S A BRIGHT EGGY HAZE IN THE SKILLET! IN 1943, RODGERS and Hammerstein (that's what those-of-us in-the-know call them) changed musical theater forever with their groundbreaking show, *Oklahoma!*, which, for the first time ever, successfully integrated song, character, plot, and dance. The story, based on Lynn Riggs' 1931 play, *Green Grow the Lilacs*, follows a young gal named Laurie who has two suitors: Curly McLain and Jud Fry. (We could make a curly fry joke here, but we won't.) There's lots of singing, lots of dancing, and a dream ballet or two. By the end, Laurie marries Curly, "pore Judd is daid," and everyone's so hungry that they're frying potatoes and topping them with eggs for breakfast. Okay, they're not really doing that, but we certainly are. This is a great weekend breakfast that you can put together faster than it takes to sing "Kansas City." Just be sure to take the time to get your potatoes really good and brown before adding the rest of the ingredients. Oh, what a beautiful morning, indeed.

4 pieces bacon (we like
    Nueske's), cut into
    lardons
1 teaspoon canola oil
3 large Russet potatoes,
    scrubbed and cut into
    ½-inch cubes

Kosher salt
Freshly ground black
    pepper
½ red onion, chopped
½ red pepper, seeded and
    chopped

1 bunch scallions, stems
    removed, thinly sliced,
    green and white parts
    separated
1 tablespoon butter
4 large eggs
Hot sauce (optional)

1. In a large cast-iron skillet, add the bacon and oil (it will help the fat render), and turn up the heat to medium. Cook the bacon, allowing the fat to seep out, until the bacon is crisp. Using a slotted metal spatula, lift the bacon into a small bowl, leaving behind the fat in the skillet.

2. See how much fat remains in the skillet, and if there's not at least ¼ cup, supplement with the oil. Crank the heat to high and carefully add the potatoes. Sprinkle with a tablespoon of kosher salt, a teaspoon of pepper, and stir all around, so all the potatoes are coated.

3. Cook the potatoes, stirring every few minutes, until the potatoes are browned all over, about 15 minutes.

RECIPE CONTINUES

4. Stir in the onion, red pepper, and the white parts of the scallions, plus another teaspoon of salt. The vegetables will give off moisture as they cook so keep stirring and frying, until the vegetables start to brown and a knife goes through a potato easily. As a final step, spread everything out and allow everything to sizzle for 30 seconds to 1 minute, to brown even more. Take the pan off the heat and stir the bacon back in. It should stay warm from the heat of the cast iron.

5. In a nonstick skillet, add the tablespoon of butter and heat on medium-high heat until foamy. Crack the eggs into a bowl and slide into the skillet (or, if you're brave, crack directly into the skillet), sprinkle with salt and pepper, and fry until the whites are just set and the yolks still look runny.

6. To serve: Scoop the fried potatoes into bowls, top each with an egg, the green parts of the scallions, and a squiggle of hot sauce (if using).

COOKING NOTES

 If your egg whites aren't setting, think of the skillet like a surrey and put a fringe (aka a lid) on top. Cook that way just until the egg whites set (about one verse of "People Will Say We're in Love").

 If you like your food spicy, you could add a chopped jalapeño (or other spicy pepper) along with the red onion and red pepper. We promise it won't be a scandal! Or an outrage!

LISTENING NOTES

 Ali Stroker won the Tony Award for Best Featured Actress in a Musical for her delectable performance as Ado Annie in the 2019 revival of *Oklahoma!*. Did you know that she is not only the first actress who uses a wheelchair to be on Broadway, but is also the first to be nominated for a Tony and also win?

 One of *Oklahoma!'s* most popular songs, the eponymously named "Oklahoma," was adopted by the actual state of Oklahoma as its official state song in 1953. They heard it and were like, "We c'aint say no!"

 Did you know that the original Dream Ballet was 18 minutes? Can you imagine not speaking for that long? Or worse . . . not eating?

Eggs to Normal

Who's Crazy? Scrambled Eggs

• • •

Inspired by NEXT TO NORMAL

Music by Tom Kitt, *Book and Lyrics by* Brian Yorkey

Opened on Broadway in 2009 at the Booth Theatre

PERFECT FOR YOU, THESE SCRAMBLED EGGS COULD BE PERFECT for you. *Next to Normal* tells the story of Diana Goodman, a suburban housewife suffering from bipolar disorder. Haunted by losing her eldest son as a baby, Diana now sees his ghost everywhere in the form of a sexy foreboding teenager in boxer shorts. But ultimately, this isn't a lusty ghost story—it's a touching and aching tale of acceptance, mental illness and all. These eggs capture the hyperactive whirlwind of Diana's mind: This is your brain on caramelized onions, bacon, eggs, cheese, and herbs. Like a good therapist, be sure to take your time dealing with the caramelized onions; they not only add a ton of flavor, they keep everything moist, even if you happen to overcook your eggs. We promise: It's gonna be good.

RECIPE CONTINUES

1 teaspoon olive oil

3 strips bacon, cut into ½-inch lardons

1 yellow onion, peeled and thinly sliced

Kosher salt

6 organic eggs

1 tablespoon whole milk

½ teaspoon freshly ground black pepper

½ cup shredded white cheddar

½ cup chopped fresh herbs (parsley, cilantro, dill, chives)

Buttered toast (for serving)

1. Add the olive oil and bacon to a nonstick skillet, heat on high heat, and when it starts sizzling, lower to medium and cook, slowly, until all the fat renders out and the bacon is crispy brown (5 to 7 minutes). Use a slotted spatula to lift the bacon onto a paper towel–lined plate, leaving the fat in the pan.

2. Add the onion to the skillet with the bacon fat, sprinkle with a little salt, and stir to coat over high heat. When the onion is sizzling and starting to brown, lower the heat to the lowest setting and cook, another 30 to 45 minutes, until the onion is a deep, golden brown.

3. Meanwhile, whisk the eggs with the milk, a teaspoon of salt, and the pepper. Add the eggs to the onion in the skillet, turn the heat up to medium-high, and fold with a heatproof rubber spatula until large curds begin to form. Add the cheese, three-quarters of the herbs, and half of the bacon back in, stir all around, and just as the eggs set, scoop onto plates. Sprinkle the remaining bacon and herbs on top and serve with the buttered toast.

COOKING NOTES

 If your superman and invisible girl are vegetarians, it's easy to make this without the bacon: Just use more olive oil at the beginning. Add 3 tablespoons—enough to coat the whole onion—and proceed with the rest of the recipe.

 Do you like softer, more custardy curds? Lower the heat when you add the eggs and cook, stirring all the while, until the eggs set (it'll take longer, about 20 minutes or so on the lowest heat). Conversely, if you like harder eggs, crank the heat up, and work fast. If you don't know which you like (YOU DON'T KNOW!?!?), just follow the original recipe.

LISTENING NOTES

 Alice Ripley stunned Broadway with her haunting portrayal of Diana Goodman, and went on to win the Tony Award for Best Actress in a Musical in 2009. Alice played the part Off-Broadway, out of town, on Broadway, and on its U.S. tour, which means she played the part from 2008 to 2011. That's a lot of belting through tears.

 Despite never winning the Tony Award for Best Musical, *Next to Normal* won the Pulitzer Prize for Drama in 2010, which made it the eighth musical in history to do so. Take that, Tonys!

 Brian d'Arcy James did *Next to Normal* Off-Broadway but chose not to continue when the show transferred to Broadway. Interestingly enough, this is not the only groundbreaking rock musical he did this with. Brian D'Arcy James also chose not to transfer from the Public Theater to Broadway with another little show called . . . *Hamilton*. What can we say? The guy hates transferring!

Matzah Mia!

Gimme! Gimme! Gimme! Matzah Brei with Sun-Dried Tomatoes, Olives, and Feta

• • •

Inspired by **MAMMA MIA!**

Music and Lyrics by Benny Andersson *and* Björn Ulvaeus, *Book by* Catherine Johnson

Opened on Broadway in 2001 at the Winter Garden Theatre

MATZAH BREI, HERE WE GO AGAIN! MY, MY, HOW CAN WE RESIST you? *Mamma Mia!* takes Swedish pop group ABBA's greatest hits and weaves them into an original story about a nosy girl named Sophie who reads her mother Donna's journal about one steamy summer 20 years ago. Sophie narrows down three suitors that could potentially be her father and, unbeknownst to her mother, invites them all to her wedding in hopes that her real father can walk her down the aisle. You bad, Sophie. Hijinks ensue, ABBA costumes are wheeled out, and tourists are famously dancing in the aisles. We call this a jukebox musical, by the way, which means that all the music is taken from a preexisting music catalogue (not to be confused with a juice box musical, which we just made up). One thing we're not confused about is matzah brei. It's a traditional Ashkenazi Jewish dish made by sautéing water-soaked matzah in butter until golden brown and then adding eggs to finish (sort of like carb-y scrambled eggs). For this version, we asked matzah brei if it wanted to go to Greece and it said: "I do! I do! I do!" And then, lucky for us, three potential dads showed up to the party: sun-dried tomatoes, olives, and feta. It's a Mediterranean take on a Jewish classic, like hearing "Dancing Queen" at a bar mitzvah on a cruise through the Grecian isles. You've done that before, right?

2 pieces unsalted, plain
   matzah
4 eggs
¼ teaspoon kosher salt
¼ teaspoon freshly
   ground black pepper
1 tablespoon olive oil

½ cup roughly chopped
   oil-packed sun-dried
   tomatoes, plus
   1 tablespoon sun-
   dried tomato oil
¼ cup oil-cured olives,
   pitted

¼ cup crumbled feta
   cheese (plus more if
   you love feta)
Dried oregano
   (for sprinkling)

1. Start by running the matzah under cold water until soaked through. Drain by shaking them off, then break up into irregular, half-inch pieces and set aside in a bowl.

2. In a separate bowl, whisk together the eggs, salt, and pepper.

3. In a medium nonstick skillet, heat the olive oil and the 1 tablespoon of sun-dried tomato oil over medium-high heat. Add the drained matzah pieces—they should sizzle when they hit the skillet—and stir around until starting to brown for

RECIPE CONTINUES

about 30 seconds to a minute. Add the sun-dried tomatoes, continue cooking for 30 seconds, then add the olives.

4. Pour in the eggs, lower the heat to medium, and, with a heatproof rubber spatula, stir all around. Add half of the feta and continue stirring until the eggs are just set.

5. Scoop onto plates and sprinkle with the remaining feta and dried oregano.

COOKING NOTES

 Matzah brei is a super trouper when it comes to versatility: You can make it savory like the recipe above, or serve it sweet. To do that, use butter instead of olive oil, skip the sun-dried tomatoes, olives, and feta, and when you serve it, sprinkle it with cinnamon sugar or a little honey, honey.

 Can't find matzah? Take a chance on saltines instead. They're already pretty salty, so be sure you don't let that extra ¼ teaspoon of salt slip through your fingers into the eggs.

LISTENING NOTES

 As of *Swiss Chards'* publication, *Mamma Mia!* holds the record as the ninth longest running show in Broadway history, having run 5,758 performances by the time it closed in 2015. It also holds the record for the longest running jukebox musical in Broadway history. (Not to be confused with a juice box musical, which, again, we just made up.)

 Mamma Mia!'s original Broadway director, Phyllida Lloyd, also ended up directing the film version of the musical starring *the* Meryl Streep. The film, like the Broadway show, was a massive hit, and went on to gross over $650 million. When ABBA wrote "Money, Money, Money," they meant it.

 Mamma Mia! isn't actually ABBA's first foray into Broadway musicals. In 1984, Benny Andersson and Björn Ulvaeus wrote the music for another musical called *Chess*, which was about . . . chess.

HamStilton

You'll-Be-Back Frittata with Ham and Blue Cheese

• • •

Inspired by HAMILTON

Music, Lyrics, and Book by Lin-Manuel Miranda

Opened on Broadway in 2015 at the Richard Rodgers Theatre

'M NOT THROWING AWAY MY FRITTAT! INSPIRED BY RON CHERNOW'S 2004 biography, *Alexander Hamilton*, *Hamilton* (heard of it?) tells the story of the founding fathers through rap, hip-hop, R&B, soul, pop, and classic musical theater, and ingeniously casts these historically white figures as non-white. From Hamilton's exodus from Nevis, to co-writing *The Federalist Papers*, to death by duel, and finally, to his late wife's private orphanage, this musical on paper feels like it really *shouldn't* work—and yet not only does it succeed, it has proven to be one of the most successful musicals of all time. Same with this frittata (at least according to us). Truly, though, it's as packed with exciting flavors—caramelized onions, smoked ham, punchy blue cheese—as *Hamilton* is packed with exciting songs. And it's way easier to make this frittata than it is to get a ticket to *Hamilton,* and cheaper, too.

RECIPE CONTINUES

4 tablespoons butter

1 yellow onion, thinly sliced

½ teaspoon kosher salt, plus more as needed

6 large organic eggs

½ teaspoon freshly ground black pepper

1 cup diced ham (preferably smoked)

¼ cup chopped fresh Italian parsley

2 tablespoons minced fresh chives, conserving a bit to sprinkle on top

½ cup crumbled blue cheese (preferably Stilton)

1. In a 9-inch cast-iron skillet, melt the butter on high heat until foaming, tilting the pan to coat all the sides (this will help the frittata detach later). Add the onion, and cook, stirring all around, so that the onion is coated and everything is sizzling. Cook for 3 to 5 minutes, until the onion starts to take on color. Sprinkle with the salt, lower the heat to medium-low, and cook, stirring every so often, for 45 minutes to 1 hour, until the onion is deep, golden brown and jammy.

2. Heat the oven to 425°F.

3. In a large bowl, whisk together the eggs, salt, and pepper for 30 seconds until everything is homogenous. Set aside.

4. Crank the heat back up to medium, add the ham, and toss gently with the onion to warm. Whisk the herbs into the eggs, then pour the eggs into the skillet, stirring all around to distribute everything evenly. Sprinkle on the blue cheese, crank up the heat to medium-high, and cook until the frittata begins to set on the sides.

5. Place the frittata in the oven and cook for 3 to 5 minutes, until the frittata puffs up and the center is just set. Turn on the broiler and broil the top of the frittata until you start to see some caramelization (be careful not to let it burn).

6. Remove from the oven and allow to cool for 5 minutes. Sprinkle with remaining chives and eat hot or at room-where-it-happens temperature.

=== COOKING NOTES ===

 It may seem tedious to cook an onion on low heat for **45** minutes, but trust us, a slowly caramelized onion will even satisfy those who are never satisfied. (And if you're feeling lazy, it's okay to just cook on high heat until brown—it'll just have more of a fried flavor, rather than a sweet, caramel-like flavor.)

 This frittata-making technique works equally well with different alliums (onion family, so: leeks, scallions, etc.), herbs (tarragon, rosemary, thyme), and cheeses (cheddar, Gruyère, Parmesan). The key is to cook the alliums in lots of butter so they keep the frittata moist when you broil it for color later. If you disagree that this is a great technique, let's duel.

LISTENING NOTES

 Hamilton's poppy breakup song for King George, "You'll Be Back," was actually written on Miranda's honeymoon. What can we say? The man is nonstop.

 To entertain people waiting in the lottery line, Miranda had members of the cast and other very notable Broadway performers put on a show for the queue-ers that was subsequently called #Ham4Ham. Miranda didn't want people who lost the lottery to go home without seeing a show. Maybe he also could have given them a frittata . . .

 Because of the fast-paced nature of its music, and despite its nearly three-hour run, *Hamilton* manages to get in an average of **144** words a minute! Lin, it's okay to take a break!

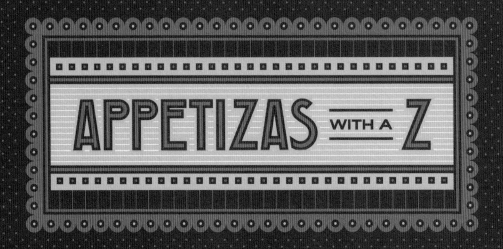

APPETIZAS WITH A Z

Cheeses Crisped Superstar

Crackers with Cheddar on Their Minds

• • •

Inspired by JESUS CHRIST SUPERSTAR

Music by Andrew Lloyd Webber, *Lyrics by* Tim Rice

Opened on Broadway in 1971 at the Mark Hellinger Theatre

EAT CHEESE CRISPS AND THEY'LL SOOTHE YOU, CALM YOU, and anoint you. The rock opera *Jesus Christ Superstar* follows the story of . . . you guessed it, Julia Child. Just kidding, Jesus Christ. Told through the eyes of that one rotten apple, Judas, and totally sung through, with not a tablespoon or ounce of a book, Jesus is essentially a hippie rockstar with a posse of apostles who adore Him. Mary washes Jesus's feet, King Herod's outrageous, Judas is pissed and screlting, they have that supper everyone's been talking about, and things really go south from there—but we don't want to give away too many spoilers. Instead, we'll give you a recipe that's super simple and super satisfying—it's a superstar!—based on a dish from the Friuli region of Italy called "frico." Essentially, it's melted cheese that firms up so that you can eat it like a cracker. We use two cheeses here: Parmesan surrounded by a halo of cheddar. And if you're wondering what that buzz is? It's cayenne pepper. Whether you serve this to your friends, apostles, or family, these crisps will have everyone singing your hosannas (unless they don't like them, in which case prepare to be CRUCIFIED).

1½ cups grated sharp
    white cheddar
1 teaspoon chopped
    fresh thyme

½ teaspoon freshly
    grated nutmeg
¼ teaspoon cayenne
    pepper

½ cup grated Parmesan
    cheese

1. Preheat the oven to 350°F. Line a baking sheet with parchment paper.

2. In a bowl, gently toss the cheddar, thyme, nutmeg, and cayenne pepper. Loosely mound tablespoon-sized mounds on the parchment paper and space them an inch apart; you should get 12. Sprinkle each with a teaspoon of the Parmesan cheese, leaving a halo of cheddar.

3. Bake for 12 to 15 minutes. The cheese will begin to bubble toward the end of cooking; keep going until it begins to brown on top. Remove from the oven and let cool completely. When cool, place on a paper towel–lined baking sheet for a minute to soak up any extra oil before serving.

RECIPE CONTINUES

Oven out of order? Try not to get worried: You can use a skillet. Heat a non-stick skillet on medium heat, add your tablespoons of cheese with the Parmesan on top, and allow them to crisp up in the skillet. Flip over when it's golden brown on the first side and finish quickly on the second side. Lift onto a paper towel–lined plate and serve as soon as they are cool and firm.

 If you've washed your hands of cheddar and Parmesan, you can make this with a variety of other cheeses, subbing a creamier cheese for the cheddar (try Montasio, Asiago, Manchego, or Gouda) and another dry cheese for the Parmesan (pecorino would work great).

LISTENING NOTES

 Andrew Lloyd Webber and Tim Rice initially couldn't get backing for their eventual mega-hit, so they released *Jesus Christ Superstar* as a musical rock album, and its success and "buzz" landed them right on Broadway.

 Did you know that there is a Chilean heavy metal band called Jesucristo Metalstar totally devoted to performing the musical at their concerts? Now you do!

 Oh my goodness, the tunes in this one. "I Don't Know How to Love Him" is a beautiful power ballad, "Heaven on Their Minds" is a rocking rock tenor opener, and blasting through the stratosphere, "Gethsemane" is Jesus's haunting cri de coeur.

Olive-r Twists

Breadsticks with "Please Sir"-ignola Olive Purée

• • •

Inspired by OLIVER!

Music, Lyrics, and Book by Lionel Bart

Opened on Broadway in 1963 at the Imperial Theatre

Y OU BETTER EAT A BREADSTICK OR TWO, YOU BETTER EAT A breadstick or two. Move over Annie and make way for the original singing orphan, Oliver! Based on Charles Dickens' 1838 novel, *Oliver Twist*, *Oliver!* tells the tale of the titular orphan who, after escaping to the city of London, is taken in by a charming kid pickpocket in a hat named the Artful Dodger, and Fagin, the elder leader of a cadre of child thieves. Oliver meets Nancy, a prostitute with a heart of gold, who is particularly taken by our little orphan (what can we say, a cherubic face with the voice of a soprano gets you *everywhere*). After a botched robbery and evading a kidnapping, Oliver moves in with a wealthy man who actually ends up being his grand-uncle, and lives happily ever after (talk about luck) while the Artful Dodger and Fagin do a jig off into the sunset. Nancy, however, doesn't have a happy ending, which is a real downer, so let's cheer ourselves up with these breadsticks. They're as simple to make as picking a pocket: just get some pizza dough, stretch it out, press in the olives, fold it in half, and cut into strips. But who will buy pizza dough when you can easily make it yourself? Good point. Any pizza dough recipe will work, especially if you sing "As Long as He *Kneads* Me" while tending to the dough. (Sorry, not sorry.)

RECIPE CONTINUES

¼ cup olive oil

2 garlic cloves, minced

¼ teaspoon red chili flakes

8 ounces (½ pound) pizza dough (homemade, store-bought, or from your favorite pizza shop), room temperature

¼ cup olives (Cerignola, oil-packed Niçoise, or Kalamata) pitted and coarsely chopped

Maldon sea salt

1. Preheat the oven to 425°F. Line two baking pans with parchment paper.

2. Stir together the olive oil, garlic, and chili flakes and set aside.

3. Roll out the pizza dough to a 10-by-12-inch rectangle—you may need some additional flour for this. Scatter and press in the olives and brush on some of the garlic oil. Fold the dough in half lengthwise, press down (some oil may sploosh around, that's okay), and then brush on the rest of the oil. Sprinkle with about a teaspoon sea salt. Cut the pizza dough crosswise into 12 one-inch strips.

4. Pick up each strip and stretch it a little, then twist it. Lay them on the baking sheet and bake for 20 minutes or until golden brown, flipping halfway through. Allow to cool to room temperature before serving.

=== COOKING NOTES ===

 Please sir, may I have some more options for these breadsticks? Okay: Try making them with lots of herbs, like chopped fresh rosemary, thyme, and/or oregano. Or sprinkle on some Parmesan cheese before baking for some extra flavor and color.

 If you have extra pizza dough and would rather make an olive-r pizza than an olive-r twist, that's a fine, fine idea. Just stretch the dough out like you did earlier to a 9-by-13-inch rectangle, brush on the garlic-chili oil, press in the olives, and add some halved cherry tomatoes, anchovies, and Parmesan cheese. Bake until the dough is dark brown and crispy, about 8 minutes.

=== LISTENING NOTES ===

 Oliver! only nabbed three Tony Awards, not even winning Best Musical, when it premiered on Broadway in 1962. However, it fared much better as a film adaptation in 1968, where it took home six Academy Awards, including Best Picture. Where is love? Guess it wasn't on Broadway.

 Did you know that the actor playing Bill Sikes in the film, Oliver Reed, was actually the nephew of the director, Carol Reed?

 In 2008, Andrew Lloyd Webber produced a reality show in the UK called "I'd Do Anything" where contestants vied weekly for the part of Nancy on the West End. Though Samantha Barks and Jesse Buckley did not end up winning, they both went on to have hugely successful careers. Samantha ended up playing Éponine in the *Les Miserables* film adaption and Jesse garnered an Academy Award nomination for Best Supporting Actress for her performance in *The Lost Daughter.*

Weenie Todds

Mini Meat Pies with Thrice-Ground Sausage and the Devil's Ketchup

• • •

Inspired by SWEENEY TODD

Music and Lyrics by Stephen Sondheim, *Book by* Hugh Wheeler

Opened on Broadway in 1979 at the Uris Theatre

FEEL YOU, MINI-MEAT PIES, I FEEL YOU. BASED ON THE PENNY dreadful, *The String of Pearls*, published in a weekly magazine from 1846 to 1847, *Sweeney Todd* follows Sweeney Todd, née the barber Benjamin Barker, who returns to London to exact his revenge on Judge Turpin. Turpin banished Todd years ago on false pretenses in order to move in on Todd's wife and now lusts after Todd's daughter, Johanna, unbeknownst to Todd. Talk about high steaks, er, stakes. Speaking of steaks, Sweeney meets Mrs. Lovett, a charming creature who seems like she must eat spiders and convinces him to make meat pies out of everyone he murders on his road to revenge. And thus, a bustling pie business is born (think *Waitress* but with cannibalism). Did all that make you hungry? Good! Here's our version of a Sweeney Todd meat pie that uses store-bought puff pastry and pre-ground Italian sausage meat so you don't have to chop up any Pirellis. The epiphany here is the Devil's Ketchup: bold and spicy, just like the musical itself. It's bound to cast a witch's spell, with smoke that comes from the mouth of hell (don't worry, that's just the cayenne). You'll be telling the tale of Weenie Todds to everyone you know.

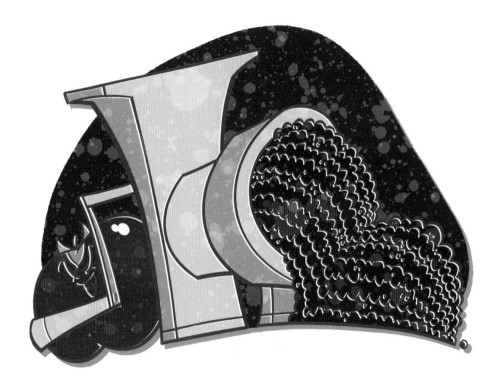

FOR THE DEVIL'S KETCHUP

¼ cup extra-virgin olive oil

1 tablespoon whole
    mustard seeds

1 tablespoon ground
    cumin

1 tablespoon ground
    coriander

1 teaspoon cinnamon

1 teaspoon allspice

¼ teaspoon ground cloves

¼ teaspoon cayenne
    pepper (more if you
    want it more devilish)

1 tablespoon minced
    fresh ginger

4 garlic cloves, minced

¼ cup apple cider vinegar

One 28-ounce can
    crushed tomatoes

¼ cup dark brown sugar

1 tablespoon kosher salt

FOR THE MEAT PIES

Flour, for dusting

1 pound frozen puff
    pastry, defrosted

¼ cup grainy mustard

1 pound sweet Italian
    sausage meat, out of
    the casing

1 egg, beaten

¼ cup sesame seeds

RECIPE CONTINUES

TO MAKE THE DEVIL'S KETCHUP

1. In a pot, gently heat the olive oil on medium heat for 30 seconds, then add the mustard seeds, cumin, coriander, cinnamon, allspice, cloves, and cayenne. Stir with a heatproof rubber spatula and cook 30 seconds to 1 minute until fragrant. Add the ginger and garlic and cook 30 seconds more.

2. Add the cider vinegar—careful of the fumes!—stir that in, and when it mostly evaporates, add the tomatoes, brown sugar, and salt. Bring to a boil, lower to a simmer, and cook for 50 minutes or so until the ketchup is thick. Taste for salt.

TO MAKE THE MEAT PIES

1. Heat the oven to 425°F and line a baking sheet with aluminum foil.

2. Dust a surface with flour and remove one of the two puff pastry sheets. Dust with flour and roll out slightly to make it more pliant; then spread on half of the grainy mustard, leaving a ½-inch border. Along the longer side of the rectangle, place half of your sausage meat and shape into a log parallel to the edge, leaving ½ inch of space. Brush the perimeter of the rectangle with the egg, then roll the puff pastry from the sausage side, overlapping the sausage, until it looks like a log. Brush the log with more egg wash and sprinkle with half of the sesame seeds. With a serrated knife, cut off the ends of the log and discard; then slice the log into 2-inch pieces and place on the baking sheet. Repeat with the remaining puff pastry and sausage meat.

3. Place the baking sheet in the oven and bake for 20 to 30 minutes until the pastry is golden brown on the top and bottom and all the pastry is cooked through (it shouldn't be doughy). Serve right away with the Devil's Ketchup.

If you don't eat pork and want to make this with poultry, try greenfinch and linnet bird . . . I mean, ground chicken or turkey that you'll have to season yourself to mimic sausage meat (try ground fennel seeds, pepper, and a teaspoon of salt).

 If ketchup is more of a miracle elixir for you than mustard, make the Devil's Ketchup ahead of time, let it cool, and spread that over the puff pastry in place of the mustard.

 Sweeney Todd is one of the rare pieces of musical theater that opera houses mount and perform. The score to this musical is so complex and exquisite that *even* opera aficionados deem it worthy to sing. It has been performed as an opera in at least nine different countries.

 A 2005 revival of *Sweeney Todd,* starring Michael Cerveris and Patti LuPone, set the musical in an insane asylum. And if that's not kooky enough, all the actors on stage accompanied themselves with instruments, too! Patti played the tuba *and* the triangle. Just like Sweeney's shears, the instruments became the actors' friends.

 The lyrics to "A Little Priest" offer some of the best food wordplay in musical theater. The hilarious and disturbing repartee could convince any innocent soul to become a murderous cannibal.

Man of La Nachos

Spanish Nachos with Impossible Meat and Manchego

• • •

Inspired by MAN OF LA MANCHA

Music by Mitch Leigh, *Lyrics by* Joe Darion, *Book by* Dale Wasserman

Opened on Broadway in 1965 at the ANTA Washington Square Theatre

TO EAT THE IMPOSSIBLE MEAT, TO SCARF THE TORTILLAS AND cheese. Loosely based on Miguel de Cervantes' 17th-century novel, *Don Quixote*, *Man of La Mancha* tells the tale of Cervantes, who transforms himself into Alonso Quijano, who transforms *himself* into Don Quixote. Following? Great. Don Quixote believes he's a knight and fights windmills that he thinks are giants. He's accompanied by his right-hand man, Sancho Panza, and falls in love with a kitchen wench, Aldonza, whom he calls Dulcinea. Sweet. Quixote's family bemoans how he deludes himself and creates an elaborate plan to snap him back into the "rightful mind" of Alonso, and it almost works, but a touching reprise of "The Impossible Dream" brings him back to his beautiful insanity and then . . . he dies. You know what would revive him? A wildly decadent tray of nachos with Spanish flair. We use Impossible meat because how could we resist the pun? Also, it's good for the planet. España comes in via the smoked paprika, the Spanish olives, and the Manchego. This is no bite of woeful countenance; this is the stuff of legend. Onward to glory (and the gym to burn these off) we go!

FOR THE QUICK-PICKLED RED ONIONS AND CHILIS

½ cup cider vinegar

½ cup water

1 tablespoon granulated sugar

1 teaspoon salt

1 red onion, thinly sliced

1 red Fresno chili or jalapeño, thinly sliced

FOR THE IMPOSSIBLE MEAT SAUCE

3 tablespoons olive oil

1 onion, chopped

4 garlic cloves, chopped

1 tablespoon smoked paprika

1 teaspoon ground cumin

¼ teaspoon cayenne pepper

12 ounces Impossible ground burger

1 teaspoon salt

One 15-ounce can black beans, drained

½ cup water

FOR THE NACHOS

One 12-ounce bag tortilla chips

8 ounces grated Manchego

8 ounces grated Monterey Jack

1 cup sour cream, thinned with a tablespoon hot water

4 multicolored radishes, sliced thinly

1 cup Spanish olives, sliced thinly

Cilantro, chopped

RECIPE CONTINUES

TO MAKE THE QUICK-PICKLED RED ONIONS AND CHILIS

1. Whisk together the cider vinegar, water, sugar, and salt.

2. Add the onion and the chili, stir to coat, and set aside for at least 1 hour.

TO MAKE THE IMPOSSIBLE MEAT SAUCE

1. Heat the olive oil in a large skillet on medium-high heat and add the onion. Cook until starting to brown, about 5 minutes. Add the garlic and cook for another 30 seconds. Add the smoked paprika, cumin, and cayenne and cook until fragrant.

2. Add the Impossible meat, sprinkle with the salt, break up with a wooden spoon, and cook until starting to brown. Add the black beans and the water and cook until everything is absorbed, seasoning with salt to taste. Set aside.

TO MAKE THE NACHOS

1. Preheat the oven to 425°F. Spray a large baking sheet with cooking spray. Layer half of the bag of tortillas, top with half of the Impossible Meat Sauce, and sprinkle with half of the Manchego and Monterey Jack. Top with the remaining tortillas, the remaining Impossible Meat Sauce, and the remaining cheese. Pop in the oven and bake for 5 to 10 minutes, until the cheese is melted and bubbling.

2. Carefully remove from the oven and drizzle with the sour cream. Top with the radishes, Spanish olives, Pickled Red Onions and Chilis, and cilantro. Serve right away.

COOKING NOTES

Looking for a holy endeavor of your own? Make your tortilla chips from scratch. It's as simple as buying a package of corn tortillas, cutting them into triangles, and then frying those triangles in a shallow layer of canola oil (about ¼ inch). Heat in a large skillet to 350°F. Carefully add your triangles, one at a time, being sure not to overcrowd. Fry until golden brown on both sides, lift on to a paper towel–lined tray, and sprinkle with salt.

Prefer a little bird, little bird to Impossible meat? Buy a rotisserie chicken, shred the meat, and add to the pan instead of the Impossible meat in the recipe above, stirring to coat in the onion, garlic, and spices. Add the black beans and a cup of water and cook down until saucy.

Brian Stokes Mitchell (whom people in the know call Stokes) played Don Quixote in the 2003 Broadway revival, and for a short spell during the COVID-19 pandemic, sang "The Impossible Dream" out of his Upper West Side window every night in honor of the essential workers. Unfortunately, so many people were gathering outside to listen (lulled by the vibrations of his extraordinary vibrato) that the city had to put a stop to it for safety concerns.

 Did you know that the original lyricist of *Man of La Mancha* was the famed British poet W. H. Auden? His lyrics, however, were too poetic and didn't scan well, and some found them too damning of the rich audiences that would be paying for the luxury of seeing the show.

 The original 1965 production of *Man of La Mancha* played for 2,328 performances and played at four different theaters in New York City before taking its final bow on June 26, 1971.

Pinto the Woods

Milky White Bean Dip with Greens, Greens, and Nothing but Greens

• • •

Inspired by INTO THE WOODS

Music and Lyrics by Stephen Sondheim, *Book by* James Lapine

Opened on Broadway in 1987 at the Martin Beck Theatre

SOMETIMES YOU MAKE BEAN DIP HALFWAY THROUGH YOUR DAY. Leave it to Stephen Sondheim and James Lapine to adapt a book that analyzes fairytales through the lens of Freudian analysis (Bruno Bettelheim's 1976 *The Uses of Enchantment*). If anyone was up to the job, it was them! In *Into the Woods,* Sondheim and Lapine ingeniously take Grimm fairytale favorites like Little Red Riding Hood, Cinderella, and Jack of beanstalk fame, mix them together, have them all go on a quest to get their wish, and then have profound existential crises about them. There will be no regrets in making this bean dip, however, no matter if you make it in the first *or* second act. Be sure to use tahini as white as milk, Aleppo pepper as red as blood, lemon as yellow as corn, and olive oil as pure as gold. Creamy, zippy, and bright, this luscious and decadent bean dip is one you'd gladly trade your pet for.

Two 15-ounce cans cannellini beans

4 garlic cloves, peeled and smashed

½ cup well-stirred tahini

¼ cup extra-virgin olive oil, plus more for drizzling

¼ cup freshly squeezed lemon juice

1½ teaspoons salt

1 cup assorted herbs (any mixture of flat-leaf parsley, cilantro, dill, mint, tarragon, and/ or basil; the more

you use, the more interesting it will taste)

Aleppo pepper

Pita chips or assorted vegetables for serving (try peppers, cabbages, and celery)

1. Drain the cannellini beans and place in a food processor with the garlic, tahini, olive oil, lemon juice, and salt. Blend for a full minute until creamy. If the mixture is too stiff, you can add a tablespoon of ice water and blend to loosen it up.

RECIPE CONTINUES

2. Once the white bean dip is to your liking, add all the herbs and begin pulsing. Your goal is to get flecks of green into the white dip without turning the whole dip green.

3. Scrape into a small serving bowl, smooth the top, and drizzle with a little more olive oil. Sprinkle on Aleppo pepper and serve with the pita chips and/or assorted vegetables.

LISTENING NOTES

 Chip Zien, the original Baker in the 1987 Broadway production, did another production of *Into the Woods* in Central Park in 2012, where he played the Mysterious Man. So, in a way, he has dueted with himself on "No More," which is very impressive. Speaking of which, if you haven't listened to the song yet, be sure to have tissues on hand as profound daddy issues will indeed pop up.

 If you've only seen the Disney movie, you *must* check out the "American Playhouse" taping of the original production, too. It's incredible. Some characters who live in the Disney one die, for instance, and some meet their death a lot more tragically. We'd say comparatively the original production is a whole lot more *Grimm*.

 Did you know that Kim Crosby and Robert Westenberg, the original Cinderella and Cinderella's Prince, met while doing the show, fell in love, and got married? Let's just hope that life doesn't imitate art too much in that happy union. Hopefully there are no Bakers' Wives or Sleeping Beauties hanging around.

A Funny Thing Happened on the Way to the Foie Gras

Chicken Liver Mousse with Cognac Brandy Tonight

• • •

Inspired by A FUNNY THING HAPPENED ON THE WAY TO THE FORUM

Music and Lyrics by Stephen Sondheim, *Book by* Burt Shevelove *and* Larry Gelbart

Opened on Broadway in 1962 at the Alvin Theatre

FOIE GRAS, THEY SAY, MAKES YOU PINE AWAY, BUT YOU PINE away with an idiotic grin! Inspired by the Ancient Roman farces by Plautus (that's Sondheim for ya), *A Funny Thing Happened on the Way to the Forum* follows Pseudolus, a slave, who, in an attempt to win his freedom, tries to help his master win a virginal (phew!) courtesan's love who has already been sold to a famous warrior (different times). To say hijinks ensue would be an understatement—hijinks is the name of the game here. There are mistaken identities, doors slamming left and right, and our favorite, lots and lots of puns. And speaking of mistaken identities, here's a great way to capture the richness and decadence of very expensive foie gras by using grocery-store chicken livers that you soak in milk to help avoid any bitterness. Cook the livers just enough to get a little color on the outside, but keep them pink on the inside and you'll have a flavorful, impressive mousse to put out for when a Miles Gloriosus comes to dinner.

RECIPE CONTINUES

1 pound chicken livers
2 cups whole milk
1 teaspoon kosher salt
1 teaspoon freshly
    ground black pepper
2 tablespoons vegetable
    oil
1 shallot, finely minced

1 tablespoon chopped
    fresh thyme leaves
1 tablespoon brandy
¼ cup heavy cream
2 sticks cold unsalted
    butter, cubed
1 teaspoon balsamic
    vinegar
Zest of 1 small orange

Zest of 1 lemon
Fancy balsamic vinegar
    or Saba (boiled grape
    must), for drizzling
Maldon sea salt
Pickled red onions
    (see Cooking Notes)
Crackers for serving
    (we like Breton)
Cornichons (optional)

1. Start by soaking the chicken livers in the milk for 30 minutes (this helps the flavor later on). Drain and discard the milk.

2. Rinse the chicken livers and examine them: If you see any green bits, get rid of them with a paring knife. Pat the livers very dry with paper towels (they'll spit if wet) and then season them with the salt and pepper.

3. Heat the oil in a large skillet on high heat and, when very hot, add the livers. Your goal here is to quickly sear them on the outside without overcooking them on the inside. As soon as they start to brown, flip them and add the shallot and thyme to the

pan. Continue cooking until, cutting into a liver, it's light pink inside. At that point, carefully add the brandy to the pan, deglazing any brown bits from the bottom. Once it's evaporated, pour all the contents of the pan into a food processor.

4. Begin blending the livers and add the cream through the feed tube. Then add the cubed, cold butter a little at a time, until it's all incorporated. Lift the lid off the food processor and add the balsamic, orange zest, and lemon zest. Pulse to combine and then taste. You want big, bold flavors (it'll mellow as it chills). Chances are it will need more salt; add at least 1 teaspoon.

5. Pour the mixture into a serving bowl and cover with plastic wrap. Refrigerate for at least 4 hours—it will firm up during that time. To serve, drizzle with your fancy balsamic (it should be thick) or Saba, sprinkle with Maldon sea salt, and top with the pickled red onions. Offer crackers and cornichons on the side.

COOKING NOTES

 Never made pickled onions before? Don't be a Hysterium! Follow the instructions in Man of La Nachos (page 52), except leave out the chilis. It's just that simple.

 If the idea of chicken livers skeeves you out, you can make a vegetarian version of this with mushrooms. Just substitute 4 cups of mushrooms (they'll cook down), sautéed in butter until golden brown on all sides. The more golden you get them, the better the mousse will be. Follow the same directions and it'll be a pretty little picture for sure.

LISTENING NOTES

 "Comedy Tonight" was not the original opening number for *A Funny Thing Happened on the Way to the Forum*. The show originally opened with a number called "Love Is in the Air," which was later repurposed for the film, *The Birdcage*, and was sung by Robin Williams and Christine Baranski.

 Another attempt at an opening number, "Invocation and Instruction to the Audience," was also repurposed. This time for another Sondheim show called *The Frogs*. Recycling: Not only good for the environment, but for artists, as well.

 Every actor who has played Pseudolus on Broadway and was eligible has won the Tony Award for Best Actor in a Musical for their performance—Zero Mostel, Phil Silvers, and Nathan Lane. Not only that, but Jason Alexander performed as Pseudolus in *one* scene in *Jerome Robbins' Broadway* and, he too, won the Tony Award for Best Actor in a Musical. The first person who doesn't win that Tony for Pseudolus is going to be dreadfully embarrassed.

How to Succeed in Blinis without Really Trying

Brotherhood of Pan-cakes with Buckwheat Flour

• • •

Inspired by HOW TO SUCCEED IN BUSINESS WITHOUT REALLY TRYING

Music and Lyrics by Frank Loesser, *Book by* Abe Burrows,
Jack Weinstock, *and* Willie Gilbert

Opened on Broadway in 1961 at the 46th Street Theatre

THERE IS A BROTHERHOOD OF BLINIS, A BENEVOLENT BROTHER-hood of blinis! Based on Shepherd Mead's 1952 satirical how-to manual of the same name, *How to Succeed in Business without Really Trying* follows J. Pierrepont Finch, an ambitious window washer at the World Wide Wicket Company, who carefully follows the how-to manual called *How to Succeed . . .* and in no time at all climbs the corporate ladder and (spoiler alert!) becomes the chairman of the board. Along the way, Finch falls in love with Rosemary, a hardworking secretary, meets Hedy La Rue, a not-so-hardworking secretary, and confronts Bud Frump, a supercilious adversary who only got his job through nepotism. If you want to earn your way to the top, and not coast on family connections, whip out the buckwheat flour and make these blinis. They're perfect for those at the bottom of the ladder (topped with sour cream and inexpensive smoked fish) or those at the very top (time to break out the $10,000 caviar). They're a cinch to make—basically pancakes with a fancier name—so if it's been a long day, treat yourself to some blinis.

¾ cup buckwheat flour

¾ cup all-purpose flour

1 tablespoon granulated sugar

1 teaspoon kosher salt

½ teaspoon baking powder

¼ teaspoon baking soda

2 cups buttermilk

3 tablespoons butter, melted

2 large eggs, separated

Vegetable oil

Crème fraîche

Smoked salmon and/or caviar

Minced fresh chives

1. In a large bowl, whisk together the buckwheat flour, all-purpose flour, sugar, salt, baking powder, and baking soda. In a separate bowl, whisk together the buttermilk, melted butter, and egg yolks. Add the buttermilk mixture to the dry ingredients and mix until just combined.

2. In a separate bowl, whisk the egg whites until stiff peaks form (you can use an electric mixer, but ambitious businesspeople do it by hand). Fold the egg whites into the batter until just combined.

RECIPE CONTINUES

3. Heat the oven to 200°F. Heat a large nonstick skillet on medium-high heat and brush with enough oil just to coat. When hot, add tablespoon-sized dollops of batter and cook, adjusting the heat to make sure they don't cook too quickly. When bubbles form on the top, flip them over and finish on the second side.

4. Stack on a baking sheet and keep warm in the oven. To serve, top with a little crème fraîche, smoked salmon, and/or caviar (if you're a top-level exec), and sprinkle with chives.

COOKING NOTES

 Boss coming to dinner and short on time? Make blinis a day or two ahead and freeze them on a baking sheet: Just put them in a single layer on parchment paper, then the next morning pop into a freezer bag for storage (unless you plan to use them right away). They should last at least two months. You can warm them up in the oven at 325°F on a baking sheet for 7 to 8 minutes.

 How to succeed in serving blinis to vegetarians? Offer alternative toppings. Try pickled beets, confited onions, or roasted asparagus on top of a layer of crème fraîche.

LISTENING NOTES

 The film adaptation of *How to Succeed . . .* was soon-to-be soap star Michele Lee's film debut. (She was the replacement of the original Rosemary, Bonnie Scott, during the Broadway run.) Michele went on to star in *Knot's Landing*, a prime-time soap opera that was on the air from 1979 to 1992. She was the only performer to appear in every episode. How to Succeed in Soap Opera. Amiright?

 Several of the original Broadway songs were omitted for the film adaptation; however, you can still hear music and verbal references in the film to two of those songs, "Coffee Break" and "Paris Original."

 Rudy Vallée, the original J.B. Bigley, had a hugely successful singing career in the late 1920s to 1930s. So much so that during the rehearsal process he tried to insert his own hits into the musical to no avail. But we love that enterprising J. Pierrepont Finch spirit.

The (Cheese) Wiz

Pimento Cheese on Down the Road

• • •

Inspired by THE WIZ

Music and Lyrics by Charlie Smalls, *Book by* William F. Brown;
Featuring songs by George Faison, Timothy Graphenreed, *and* Luther Vandross,
Featuring songs with Lyrics by George Faison *and* Luther Vandross

Opened on Broadway in 1975 at the Majestic Theatre

WHEN I THINK OF PIMENTO CHEESE, I THINK OF AN APP WHERE there's love overflowing. Based on L. Frank Baum's *The Wizard of Oz*, *The Wiz* infuses R&B and soul into the beloved classic, and broke boundaries in the 1970s with an entirely Black cast leading a big budget musical on Broadway. Dorothy may still be Dorothy here, but Glinda now has a Good Witch sister named Addaperle, the Wicked Witch of the East is Evamean, and her vindictive sister ruling over the West is now Evillene. Talk about aptronyms (yes we did look that word up, and so should you). Dorothy, a cold-blooded killer, kills off both wicked sisters, and once succeeding in doing so clicks her *silver* slippers three times (a nod to the original novel—take that, Victor Fleming!) and finds herself back home where there's a big pot of pimento cheese waiting for her. Maybe that part's not true, but it'll be true for you once you make this classic Southern recipe that actually originated in the North. It's a wicked combination of sharp white cheddar, mayonnaise, and pimentos that you whizz up (get it?) in the food processor. One bite, and you'll never leave home again.

RECIPE CONTINUES

2 cups shredded sharp white cheddar (Tillamook or Cracker Barrel)

½ cup mayonnaise

½ cup jarred pimentos or roasted red peppers (liquid squeezed out)

1 garlic clove, minced

1 habanero pepper, stemmed, seeded, and finely minced (use gloves if sensitive)

A few dashes of Tabasco

1 teaspoon freshly ground black pepper

½ teaspoon kosher salt

Celery sticks or stoned wheat thins, for serving

1. In the bowl of a food processor, combine the cheddar, mayonnaise, pimentos, garlic, habanero, Tabasco, and black pepper. Blend (or whizz!) until everything is roughly combined. Taste for salt and heat (add more Tabasco if necessary). Serve with the celery sticks or stoned wheat thins.

The person who taught us this recipe, food writer Rachel Wharton, only processes three-quarters of the mixture, combining the rest with a rubber spatula. It makes the texture a little more complex if you want to enjoy your cheese a brand-new way (like a brand-new day . . . get it?).

 Pimento cheese also works as a decadent condiment. Try it on a burger or serve it with some fried chicken (see Grease (Is the Bird) on page 116). It's outrageously good, though you may need a heart transplant from the Tin Man.

 Motown Productions acquired the rights to *The Wiz* very quickly after its 1975 Broadway debut, so that its original star, Stephanie Mills, would be the right age for the part. However, 33-year-old Diana Ross had different plans for Dorothy. After being rejected for being too old for the part, Diana got Universal Pictures to agree to finance the film on the basis of her participation, thus securing the role. Diana didn't need silver slippers; she just needed silver dollars.

 The Wiz director Geoffery Holder was the first Black man to ever win the Tony Award for Best Director of a Musical and Best Costume Design of a Musical. Additionally, at the time of *Swiss Chards'* publication, Charlie Smalls is currently the only Black man to have ever won Best Original Score for his work on *The Wiz*.

 The Wiz had a hard time finding an audience in the beginning of its run, so the producers decided to advertise a segment of the deliciously catchy song "Ease on Down the Road" on TV, and in doing so, became the second Broadway show to ever have a TV commercial. This ingenious move helped the show catch fire, and the cast and crew could safely call their theater "Home."

2. Bring to a boil, then lower to a simmer and cook for 25 to 30 minutes, stirring every so often, until the lentils are tender and the soup is thick. Taste for salt and adjust with more curry powder and cayenne pepper to make the flavors as big and bold as you want them to be. Serve with dollops of Greek yogurt, cilantro leaves, and lime wedges.

COOKING NOTES

 This soup freezes really well for those cold winter nights when all you have in the kitchen is Bustelo, Marlboro, and bananas by the bunch.

 If you want to give this soup a tune-up, add a can of well-stirred coconut milk along with the tomatoes. It'll make the resulting soup silky, slightly sweet, and luscious.

LISTENING NOTES

 Jonathan Larson unfortunately never lived to see *Rent* take the world by storm. In a sad and strange confluence of events, he died from an aortic dissection on the very morning of the first preview of *Rent*'s Off-Broadway debut.

 Rent quickly became a cultural phenomenon when it premiered in 1996. It not only innovated the form, but also how it was accessed. Jeffery Seller, the show's main producer, made a limited number of discounted rush tickets available every day to *anyone* who waited in line on a first-come, first-served basis. Kids slept out on the streets to get them. Dangerous, but worth it. No, but seriously, it was dangerous, so Jeffery then invented a lottery system instead, now a Broadway staple, and democratized the whole thing.

 At the time *of Swiss Chards'* publication, *Rent* is currently one of only 10 musicals in history to have ever received the Pulitzer Prize.

3 tablespoons olive oil

1 red onion, finely chopped

1 yellow or orange pepper, finely chopped

Kosher salt

4 garlic cloves, minced

2-inch piece of ginger, peeled and minced

1 fresh habanero chili, seeded and minced (use less if you don't like heat)

1 bunch cilantro, stems thinly sliced and leaves reserved for later

1 tablespoon curry powder

½ teaspoon turmeric

¼ teaspoon cayenne pepper

1 cup brown or green lentils

One 14.5-ounce can crushed tomatoes

5 cups water

Full-fat Greek yogurt

Lime wedges

1. Heat a large pot on high heat for 30 seconds, then add the olive oil, onion, and yellow or orange pepper. Sauté, with a pinch of salt, until turning translucent (about 5 minutes). Then add the garlic, ginger, chili, and cilantro stems. Cook for another minute, until everything is softened. Then add the curry powder, turmeric, and cayenne pepper. Toast until fragrant, then add the lentils, tomatoes, and water, plus 1 teaspoon salt.

RECIPE CONTINUES

Rent-il Soup

Curried Lentil Soup with Seasonings of Love

• • •

Inspired by RENT

Music, Lyrics, and Book by Jonathan Larson

Opened on Broadway in 1996 at the Nederlander Theatre

THE EARTH TURNS, THE SUN BURNS, BUT I DIE, WITHOUT LENTIL SOUP. *Rent* loosely takes Giacomo Puccini's 1896 opera, *La Bohème*, and retools it as a rock opera, centering around impoverished artists living in the East Village in the late '90s struggling with HIV/AIDS, the conundrum of making art or selling out, and stressing out or really not stressing out *enough* about making . . . rent. Larson's groundbreaking musical is filled with pathos and extraordinary characters, and introduced to the world the most omnipresent musical theater song to ever grace a youth cabaret, choir showcase, or night at Marie's Crisis. And this lentil soup is sure to be an omnipresent regular in your kitchen for any of the 525,600 minutes of the year. The cast of ingredients is as diverse as the show itself—ginger brings Angel-like zip, habanero brings Mimi-like heat—and the resulting soup is something they'd surely serve at The Life Cafe (sorry, no meatless balls). Feel free to add more spices if you'd like (cumin, coriander, and cardamom all work); regardless, this soup is certain to take you over the moon.

RENT-IL SOUP

Curried Lentil Soup with Seasonings of Love

+ 70 +

The POKÉ HORROR SHOW

Rose-Tinted Beet Salad with Seared Tuna

+ 73 +

PORGY and WATERCRESS

Smoked Trout Salad with Summertime Herbs

+ 76 +

LITTLE CHOP of HORRORS

Somewhere-That's-Green Lettuces with Sticky Licky Beets

+ 79 +

DEAR MELON HANSEN

Summer Melon Salad, Waving Through a Prosciutto

+ 82 +

HAIR-LOOM TOMATO SALAD

Tie-Dyed Tomato Salad with Electric Blue Cheese

+ 85 +

The Poké Horror Show

Rose-Tinted Beet Salad with Seared Tuna

• • •

Inspired by THE ROCKY HORROR SHOW

Music, Lyrics, and Book by Richard O'Brien

Opened on Broadway in 1975 at the Belasco Theatre

WHY DON'T YOU STAY FOR A NIGHT? OR MAYBE A BITE? I could show you my favorite obsession . . . fake poké. An ode to the B-horror and sci-fi films of yesteryear, *The Rocky Horror Show* follows Brad and Janet as they seek refuge one night at Dr. Frank-N-Furter's mysterious old castle. Frank is a crossdressing mad scientist who is excited to show them his creation—a hottie with a body named Rocky. A *Noises Off* level of sexcapades and murders ensue, Frank and his minions are actually revealed to be aliens, Frank is murdered, and then everyone does the "Time Warp". . . again. And since we're all playing dress-up, why not dress up some beets? That's what we're doing here with this riff on poké, a Hawaiian dish, traditionally made with raw tuna, and dressed with soy sauce, sesame oil, and scallions. Here, the beets put on the tuna costume, and the tuna wears a gorgeous coat of sesame seeds. Served with rice and a sprinkle of furikake (a Japanese seaweed condiment), this is a dish that'll have everyone wanting to touch-a touch-a touch it with their fork.

RECIPE CONTINUES

6 large raw beets
(one bunch)

Kosher salt

3 tablespoons soy sauce

2 tablespoons toasted
sesame oil

2 tablespoons rice wine
vinegar

Juice of 1 lime

1 tablespoon chili crisp
(optional)

1-inch piece of ginger,
peeled and grated

1 fat garlic clove, grated

3 scallions, thinly sliced

1 cup sesame seeds

4 fillets sushi-grade
ahi tuna

Freshly ground black
pepper

3 tablespoons vegetable
or grapeseed oil

Cooked white rice,
for serving

Furikake (optional)

1. Bring a big pot of water to a boil. While that's happening, wash and peel your beets,
   then cut them into half-inch cubes to resemble cubed pieces of tuna. Salt the water
   so that it tastes like broth, then add your beets. Cook at a simmer until a knife goes
   through the beets easily—10 to 15 minutes.

2. While the beets are cooking, whisk together the soy sauce, sesame oil, rice wine
   vinegar, lime juice, chili crisp (if using), ginger, garlic, and half of the scallions.
   Taste to adjust for acid (with more rice wine vinegar) or salt (more soy sauce).

3. When the beets are cooked, drain them carefully, then toss them with the dressing.
   It will seem like a lot of liquid, but this ensures that everything marinates equally.
   Allow the beets to cool to room temperature and, if not using right away, refrigerate
   until ready to use.

4. Place the sesame seeds in a shallow dish. Pat the tuna dry with paper towels, season with salt and pepper, and then press into the sesame seed mixture to make it stick on all sides.

5. Heat the oil in a large nonstick skillet. When almost smoking, add the tuna and sear on all sides until the sesame seeds are all golden. Remove to a cutting board and slice into ¼-inch slices (it's okay if it's a bit raw in the middle, as long as the tuna is sushi-grade).

6. To serve, spoon the rice into bowls, sprinkle it with some furikake (if using), top with some of the beet mixture, and lay the slices of tuna on top. If there's any liquid left at the bottom of the beet bowl, drizzle it over the tuna. Sprinkle the tuna with the remaining scallions and then sprinkle with more furikake.

COOKING NOTES

If you can't find sushi-grade tuna, you can make this dish with seared salmon (or any other fish you like). Just forget the sesame seeds and sear the salmon until it reaches an internal temperature of 125°F (for medium-rare). No need to slice it up; this is a piece of salmon, not Eddie (RIP, Eddie).

For even more pizzazz, you could use a mixture of golden beets and red beets, but you'll want to keep them separate or else in an organic rush of lust, the red beets will rose-tint the gold beets' world.

LISTENING NOTES

Richard O'Brien, who created *The Rocky Horror Show* (and played Riff-Raff in the original London production, Broadway production, and film adaptation), was actually an out-of-work actor at the time and wrote the piece to quell his boredom, which reminds us of the phrase "boredom is the mother of invention . . . "

The original running time of the show was only 40 minutes, so O'Brien created its most famous song "Time Warp" to pad out the show, which reminds us of the phrase "a short running time is the mother of invention . . ."

The musical's film adaptation, *The Rocky Horror Picture Show*, became a cult classic and holds the Guinness World Record for longest continuously running theatrical release in the United States. Before the pandemic, it was shown continuously for over 40 years at the Oriental Theater in Milwaukee, which reminds us of the phrase "a continuous—" (Okay, this is exhausting).

Porgy and Watercress

Smoked Trout Salad with Summertime Herbs

• • •

Inspired by PORGY AND BESS

Music by George Gershwin, *Lyrics by* DuBose Heyward *and* Ira Gershwin, *Libretto by* DuBose Heyward

Opened on Broadway in 1935 at the Alvin Theatre

WATERCRESS AND THE EATIN' IS EASY, SMOKED TROUT ARE jumpin', and the grapes are sliced. Based on Heyward's 1927 play, *Porgy*, which is adapted from his 1925 novel of the same name (show off), *Porgy and Bess* tells the story of, well, Porgy and Bess. Porgy is a disabled beggar who falls in love with Bess, a drug-addicted prostitute, and tries to save her from the grasp of her pimp and lover, Crown, and her drug dealer, Sportin' Life. It's a roaring musical comedy. Just kidding, it's really not. Though this musical—or opera, a hot debate—has been criticized for its stereotypical portrayals of Black Americans (for example, Harry Belafonte refused to be in the film version because he deemed it "racially demeaning"), in 1935 it innovated the Broadway scene by featuring a predominantly Black cast. The most famous song in it, "Summertime," is the prompt for this summery mix of peppery arugula, cucumbers, smoked trout (aka porgy), and lots of herbs. Feel free to recast some of the ingredients: plums would work great instead of grapes, as would nectarines. And if you've got plenty of nothin', just the arugula and smoked trout can make a tasty lunch.

4 cups baby arugula
(or any other bitter
lettuce)

1 English cucumber,
peeled, thinly sliced

1 cup red seedless
grapes, sliced in half

4 scallions, sliced thin
(white and green
parts)

½ cup chopped almonds,
toasted

½ teaspoon salt

¼ teaspoon pepper

¼ cup extra-virgin olive oil

2 tablespoons white wine
vinegar

1 smoked trout fillet
(¼ pound), shredded

3 tablespoons chopped,
fresh summertime
herbs (including basil,
tarragon, mint, dill,
etc.)

1. In a large bowl, toss together the arugula, cucumber, grapes, scallions, half of the almonds, salt, and pepper. Then drizzle in the olive oil and vinegar, and toss again. Add the shredded trout fillet and half of the herbs and toss again.

2. Serve in two chilled bowls with the remainder of the almonds and herbs sprinkled over the top.

RECIPE CONTINUES

This salad isn't exclusive to summertime: You can find arugula and grapes all year long. If it *is* summertime though, you can make this even more summery by adding chunks of watermelon or other melons and lots of basil and using multicolored cherry tomatoes instead of the grapes.

 If you want a more emulsified dressing, add a tablespoon of Dijon mustard, whisk in the vinegar, then slowly whisk in the olive oil. This makes the dressing slightly heavier, so Dijon is just a sometime thing.

 Gershwin was so smitten by Anne Brown (the original Bess and first Black vocalist to be admitted to Julliard) that he greatly enlarged the part of Bess. He not only kept writing her more and more songs but changed the name of the opera from *Porgy* to *Porgy AND Bess*.

 "Summertime," a gorgeous aria, is the most well-known song from the show's catalogue, and is actually the most covered song in the history of recorded music, having been covered over 33,000 times! So do some digging and pick your favorite version because we *do not* pick favorites over here.

 Over the course of the two-year development of *Porgy and Bess*, the Gershwins and Heyward collaborated mostly by mail, rarely meeting in person. So you can thank those snail mail collaborations for hits like "Summertime," "I Got Plenty O' Nuttin'," and "It Ain't Necessarily So."

Little Chop of Horrors

Somewhere-That's-Green Lettuces with Sticky Licky Beets

• • •

Inspired by LITTLE SHOP OF HORRORS

Music by Alan Menken, *Book and Lyrics by* Howard Ashman

Opened on Broadway in 2003 at the Virginia Theatre

C ALL A COP, YUMMY BEET CHOPPED SALAD, YUM, YUM, YUM, MMM! Loosely based on the 1960 movie of the same name, *Little Shop of Horrors* follows Seymour Krelborn, a hapless and meek florist, who raises Audrey II, a talking, man-eating plant from outer space, hell-bent on world domination. Have we mentioned this is also a musical? *Little Shop of Horrors* is chock-full of some of the catchiest songs in the canon, thoroughly memorable characters, and loads of dentist jokes (hopefully that's your thing!). This salad is light enough for an Audrey I to keep her figure and meat-packed enough for an Audrey II not to complain. And the beets lend a certain gory undercurrent that's one part nutrient-packed power vegetable and one part partially digested dentist. Alright, it's suppertime.

RECIPE CONTINUES

FOR THE SALAD

1 bunch red beets (3 or 4 beets), tops and roots removed, scrubbed clean

3 tablespoons extra-virgin olive oil

1 teaspoon kosher salt

½ teaspoon freshly ground black pepper

4 strips smoked bacon

3 tablespoons honey

1 tablespoon lemon juice

2 heads romaine, cleaned and chopped

½ red onion, thinly sliced

1 English cucumber, peeled, seeded, and chopped

One 15-ounce can chickpeas, drained

½ cup, crumbled imported feta or goat cheese

FOR THE DRESSING

1 tablespoon Dijon mustard

1 teaspoon honey

3 tablespoons sherry vinegar

½ teaspoon kosher salt

½ teaspoon freshly ground black pepper

½ cup extra-virgin olive oil

1. Heat the oven to 375°F. Peel the beets and chop into ½-inch chunks. Toss with the olive oil, salt, and pepper, and place on a foil-lined baking sheet. Pop in the oven and roast, tossing the beets occasionally for 30 minutes, or until a knife goes through a beet easily.

2. While you're roasting the beets, you can cook the bacon in the oven. On a baking sheet lined with foil and sprayed with cooking spray, set the four pieces of bacon. Place directly in the oven, and bake until the bacon is crisp and most of the fat is rendered, about 15 minutes. Carefully remove from the oven (beware of the hot fat!), pour the fat into a bowl for a separate use (great for scrambling eggs or frying potatoes), and allow the bacon to cool.

3. Remove the beets from the oven and, in a large bowl, toss the warm beets with the honey and lemon juice. Return them to the baking sheet and roast, keeping an eye on them, until the beets look glossy and glazed, another 5 minutes. Remove from the oven and allow the beets to cool.

4. To make the dressing, whisk the mustard, honey, vinegar, salt, and pepper together. Slowly whisk in the oil and allow the dressing to emulsify. Dip a finger in and taste: too tart? Add more honey. Too bland? Add a little more salt.

5. In a large bowl, toss the lettuce, onion, cucumber, and chickpeas by hand with a teaspoon of salt. Add the beets, crumble in the bacon, and slowly add the dressing, tossing thoroughly with your hands, tasting as you go. Add as much dressing as you need to lightly coat the vegetables, but not so much that the salad becomes soggy.

6. Add the crumbled feta, toss again, and serve immediately in deep salad bowls, with a little more feta crumbled on top and lots of freshly ground black pepper.

COOKING NOTES

 If you're as insatiable as Audrey II, you could use the bacon fat to make the dressing. Allow the fat to cool slightly and use an equal amount of it instead of the olive oil when whisking.

 Feta works nicely because it's punchy enough to make an impact but subtle enough not to dominate like the monstrous Orin Scrivello, DDS. If you're looking for something more assertive, try making this with Gorgonzola.

LISTENING NOTES

 You might find some of these tunes quite recognizable, as this is the same writing team that brought you *The Little Mermaid*, *Aladdin*, and *Beauty and the Beast*. Menken also went on to write every other musical you've ever loved: *Newsies*, *Hercules*, *Hunchback of Notre Dame*, *Pocahontas*, *Enchanted*, *Tangled*, and many more. Basically, you and your parents should be deeply grateful for all the babysitting this duo has done.

 Alan Menken's father was actually a dentist, and like a good Jewish mother, his mother bemoaned that he was breaking her heart with his song "Dentist." Both authors of this book happen to be sons of dentists, too. (And Jewish mothers.)

 There are so many hits to look out for in this cast album, most specifically: "Somewhere That's Green," "Grow for Me," and "Suddenly Seymour."

Dear Melon Hansen

Summer Melon Salad,
Waving Through a Prosciutto

• • •

Inspired by DEAR EVAN HANSEN

Music and Lyrics by Benj Pasek *and* Justin Paul, *Book by* Steven Levenson

Opened on Broadway in 2016 at the Music Box Theatre

ALL WE SEE IS MELON WRAPPED IN PROSCIUTTO, FEELS LIKE WE could go on forever this way. *Dear Evan Hansen* follows a well-meaning, awkward teenager named Evan Hansen, who gaslights a grieving family into believing that he was great friends with their son who just died by suicide (typical high-school fare). Evan fills the family's aching void, moves in on their daughter, and finds a father figure he's never had. All goes well except when Evan's crippling anxiety over his guilty conscience causes his lies to spiral out of control. You should think of the prosciutto in this dish as the lies spiraling around Evan's sweet melon heart. With a base of whipped ricotta that represents the sky (just go with it), this is a salad that features peak summer fruit in the most luscious, surprising way. The prosciutto gives a surprising meaty crunch, the ricotta adds creaminess and heft, and the herbs help seal the deal that this is an appetizer and not a dessert. Although a dessert pretending to be an appetizer is very Evan Hansen.

6 slices prosciutto

12 ounces fresh ricotta (we like Bellwether Farms)

2 tablespoons heavy cream

½ teaspoon kosher salt, plus more for later

A very heavy, fragrant melon (honeydew or cantaloupe), peeled, seeded, and sliced into thick wedges

2 peaches, sliced into thick wedges

¼ cup extra-virgin olive oil

Maldon sea salt

Freshly ground black pepper

Lots of chopped summer herbs (about 3 tablespoons): basil, tarragon, dill, parsley (whichever you can find)

1. Preheat your oven to 325°F and lay the prosciutto on a parchment-lined baking sheet. Bake for 15 to 20 minutes, flipping the prosciutto halfway, until the prosciutto looks crisp. Remove from the oven and allow to cool.

2. In a stand mixer with the whisk attachment, work the ricotta with the heavy cream and salt until light and fluffy—about 1 minute.

3. Spoon the ricotta onto four chilled plates. Arrange the melon and peaches on top, drizzle with the olive oil, sprinkle with Maldon sea salt and pepper, and scatter the herbs all over the top. Lean a crisp prosciutto against the side of each melon-peach stack and serve right away.

RECIPE CONTINUES

How do you peel a melon? It's sort of like breaking in a glove. (Is it? We don't know. We've never played sports. We're Broadway cookbook authors.) Slice off the top and bottom of the melon and, with a very sharp chef's knife, follow the shape of the melon as you slice off the skin the way you would with an orange. Alternatively, you can just slice the melon into wedges and cut the melon off the skin by gliding along the arc of the melon wedge.

 Whipped ricotta is such a great trick to have up your sleeve that words fail to describe it. Try it on toasted country bread with a drizzle of olive oil or as a dip with lots of summery vegetables, and you will be found to be a great chef.

 Ben Platt, who took the world by storm for his moving portrayal of Evan Hansen, is one of the youngest men (or should we say boys?) to ever receive the Tony Award for Best Performance by a Leading Actor in a Musical for his work in *Dear Evan Hansen*. He was only 23!

 Did you know that four successive actors playing Evan Hansen have dated each other? Noah Galvin replaced Ben Platt and then they started canoodling. Taylor Trensch came in after Galvin and then started dating Ben Levi Ross who was his understudy (and then went on to play Evan on the US tour and on Broadway). Maybe we should have put dates in this recipe.

 Despite ushering in two Tony Award–winning best musicals, *Rent* and *Dear Evan Hansen,* and two Pulitzer Prize–winning musicals, *Rent* and *Next to Normal*, *Evan Hansen*'s director, Michael Greif, has never brought home the Tony Award for Best Director of a Musical. People in the know call him the Glenn Close of Broadway. (No one has ever called him that.)

Hair-Loom Tomato Salad

Tie-Dyed Tomato Salad with Electric Blue Cheese

• • •

Inspired by **HAIR**

Music by Galt MacDermot, *Lyrics and Book by* Gerome Ragni *and* James Rado

Opened on Broadway in 1968 at the Biltmore Theatre

GLIDDY GLOOP GLOOPY NIBBY NOBBY NOOBY LA LA LA LO tomato salad. With those lyrics (minus the tomato salad), the first rock musical was born! *Hair* tells the story of Claude, Berger, and Sheila, and their tribe of long-haired hippies in the '60s who defy the draft, espouse pacifism, and get buck naked. Will Claude abide by his conservative parents and go off to fight in Vietnam or will he stay with his hippie family in NYC and get buck naked? We don't know about Claude, but, for us, it's much easier to get buck naked if we have a salad for dinner. This one is a summery be-in of bright colors and flavors. Use the freshest, ripest tomatoes and peaches/plums/nectarines you can find and feel free to experiment. Ain't got no olives? Use capers. Ain't got no blue cheese? Use feta. It's easy to be hard on yourself when you make a salad, but here's our conviction: Buy peak summer produce and you'll let the sunshine in.

RECIPE CONTINUES

4 large, ripe multicolored heirloom tomatoes

2 to 3 ripe peaches, plums, or nectarines

3 small Persian cucumbers, thinly sliced

1 small red onion, thinly sliced

¼ cup oil-cured black olives, pitted

¼ cup best-quality extra-virgin olive oil (we like Seka Hills or Katz)

1 teaspoon Maldon sea salt

½ teaspoon freshly ground black pepper

1 tablespoon best-quality balsamic vinegar (as syrupy as you can find it)

½ cup (4 ounces) crumbled blue cheese (Roquefort or Danish blue)

Fresh basil leaves (about 6), chiffonaded (see Cooking Notes)

1 bunch dill, roughly chopped

1. Using a small serrated knife, cut the cores out of the tomatoes and then cut the tomatoes into irregular pieces: wedges, slices, chunks, squares. The shapes should be interesting and easy to pick up on a fork. Cut the peaches, plums, or nectarines into similarly sized shapes and arrange everything on a platter.

2. Lay on the cucumbers, onion, and half of the olives. Drizzle with the olive oil, then sprinkle with the salt and pepper. Drizzle with the balsamic, then sprinkle the blue cheese and the remaining olives on top. Garnish with the basil leaves and dill.

Want us to roll you one, man? No, not that, we're talking about basil rolled up so that you can chiffonade. Just lay basil leaves on top of each other (4 or 5), roll them up tightly, and then slice. You should get strips of fresh basil. That's a chiffonade!

 How do you know if a tomato is ripe? Don't squeeze it: Your finger might go through it (aka the flesh failures). Instead, just hold it and if it's very heavy, that tomato is ready to go.

LISTENING NOTES

 Ragni and Rado, who wrote *Hair*, also originated the roles of Claude and Berger, but there was another notable actor in that cast: Diane Keaton. Heard of her?

 Hair was truly revolutionary for its time. Broadway had never seen a musical quite like it. Just to give you perspective of how anomalous it was, when *Hair* opened, musicals like *Hello, Dolly!*, *Man of La Mancha*, *Funny Girl*, and *Fiddler on the Roof* were all still playing.

 When Melba Moore assumed the role of Sheila after Lynn Kellogg finished her run, Melba made Broadway history by being the first Black person to ever take over a role originated by a white person without changing the show to an all-Black cast.

THREE PENNE OPERA

Baked Pasta with Pirate Genoese Pesto, Garlicky Tomatoes, and Mozzarella

+ 90 +

VELVITA

Chorizo Mac and Ché-ese

+ 94 +

CATS-EROLE

Tuna Casserole with Frizzabella Onions

+ 97 +

CRABARET

Crab Cakes with Two-Ladles-of-Garlic Aioli

+ 100 +

The CLAM'S VISIT

Clams from Papi's Ocean with Preserved Lemons on Israeli Couscous

+ 103 +

CODSPELL

Poached Cod with Mussels and All Good Gifts

+ 106 +

SPRING A-WOK-ENING

Stir-Fried Spring Vegetables with Totally Plucked Chicken

+ 109 +

CHICKEN BREAST SIDE STORY

Pineapple Maria-nated Chicken Breast with Fried Plantains and Sazón Rice

+ 112 +

GREASE (IS the BIRD)

Summer-Lovin' Fried Chicken with Hot Honey

+ 116 +

HEDWIG and the ANGRY SANDWICH

Pig-in-a-Box Pulled Pork Sliders

+ 120 +

SUNDAY in the PORK with GEORGE

Color-and-Light Pork Meatballs in Tomato Sauce

+ 124 +

SHE LOAFS ME

Will He Like Me-atloaf with Vanilla Bean Mashed Sweet Potatoes

+ 128 +

The SOUND of MOUSSAKA

Eggplant and "Lonely Goatherd" Lamb Casserole

+ 132 +

CAULIFLOWER DRUM SONG

A Hundred Million Granules of Cauliflower Fried "Rice"

+ 136 +

DREAMGRILLS

One Bite–Only Mushroom Kabobs with You're-Gonna-Sesame Sauce

+ 139 +

Three Penne Opera

Baked Pasta with Pirate Genoese Pesto, Garlicky Tomatoes, and Mozzarella

• • •

Inspired by THE THREEPENNY OPERA

Music by Kurt Weill, *Lyrics and Book by* Bertolt Brecht

Opened on Broadway in 1933 at the Empire Theatre

O H, THE BAKED PASTA HAS TOMATOES, DEAR, AND HE SHOWS them dripping in cheese. Based on John Gay's 18th-century opera, *The Beggar's Opera*, *The Threepenny Opera* was originally called "a play with music," but that's just because musicals didn't exist yet. (In fact, with *The Threepenny Opera*, Weill and Brecht are frequently given credit as the creators of one of the first widely known musicals.) A socialist critique on capitalism, the show follows Macheath who marries the Beggar King's daughter, Polly, much to the Beggar King's chagrin. The Beggar King orchestrates Mack's murder, but Mack has friends in high places and thwarts the Beggar King's plan and all live happily ever after. Except the beggars . . . because capitalism rots. If that was too complicated, here's a baked pasta dish that's not. A Genoese pesto, with basil and garlic, gets folded into penne, topped with a mix of cherry tomato sauce and lots of cheese, then baked in the oven until it's crispy on top. Sort of like an Italian mac and cheese, this is a meal that'll quell the angry hordes; for, after all, even honest folk may act like sinners, unless they've had their customary dinners.

FOR THE PESTO

¼ cup pine nuts, lightly
   toasted in a dry skillet
   (see Cooking Notes)

4 fat garlic cloves, peeled

2 big bunches (about
   4 loosely packed cups)
   fresh basil leaves

½ teaspoon kosher salt

¾ cup extra-virgin olive
   oil

1 cup freshly grated
   Parmesan cheese

**FOR THE GARLICKY
TOMATOES**

2 tablespoons extra-virgin
   olive oil

4 fat garlic cloves, sliced
   thin

1 tablespoon tomato
   paste

Pinch red chili flakes

2 cups cherry tomatoes,
   stems removed

½ teaspoon salt

½ cup water

FOR THE BAKED PASTA

Kosher salt

1 pound dried penne

½ cup freshly grated
   Parmesan cheese

8 ounces shredded
   mozzarella

Basil leaves, chiffonaded
   (optional), to serve

RECIPE CONTINUES

TO MAKE THE PESTO

1. Preheat the oven to 425°F.

2. In the bowl of a food processor, combine the toasted pine nuts, garlic, basil leaves, and salt, and pulse several times until it resembles a paste. Slowly drizzle in the olive oil, pulsing all the way, until the mixture is more saucy, but not homogenous (leave it a bit chunky). Pour the pesto into a large heatproof bowl, and fold in the Parmesan cheese.

TO MAKE THE GARLICKY TOMATOES

1. In a skillet, heat the olive oil with the garlic and tomato paste. Cook until garlic is starting to turn golden and the tomato paste turns rust-colored. Add the chili flakes, cherry tomatoes, salt, and water.

2. Stir all around on high heat until bubbling, cover with a lid, and cook for several minutes until all the tomatoes burst (you can crush them with a wooden spoon, if necessary). Lift the lid off and cook until the tomato sauce is thick. Set aside.

TO MAKE THE BAKED PASTA

1. Season a large pot of boiling water with a few tablespoons of kosher salt to make it taste like good chicken broth, but not so much salt that it tastes like seawater. Cook your dried penne until just al dente, one minute less than package directions. Strain (don't rinse!) and place into the bowl with the pesto, stirring everything together.

2. Grease a large cast-iron skillet or 9-by-13-inch baking pan with olive oil and add half of your pesto pasta. Spoon on half of the garlicky tomatoes, scattering them over the top, then sprinkle with half of the Parmesan and half of the mozzarella. Cover with the remaining pasta, the remaining garlicky tomatoes, the Parmesan, and the mozzarella.

3. Bake in the oven for 30 minutes, until the cheese is melted and starting to brown and crispy around the edges. Allow to cool for several minutes before serving with the optional basil garnish.

To toast pine nuts evenly, you can either spread them out on a baking sheet and roast in a 350°F oven until golden brown all over (the safest way); or, if you like things dangerous (appropriate for this musical), place the pine nuts in a small metal skillet and crank the heat up to medium. Toss as they warm up and keep a close eye on them. When they start to turn golden, 3 to 4 minutes, immediately remove them to a bowl to cool.

 Instead of pine nuts (which are way expensive), you can make this recipe with almonds, walnuts, or pistachios. Just toast them the same way and you're good to go.

 Lucky for us we have an actor's tantrum to thank for *The Threepenny Opera*'s most famous song. Right before its Berlin premiere, Harald Paulsen, the original Macheath, threatened to leave the show if his character didn't get a proper introduction, and thus, "Mack the Knife" was born.

 In 1956, Lotte Lenya, who also played the part of Jenny in the 1931 film adaptation and was married to the show's composer, Kurt Weill, won a Tony Award for her performance in the Off-Broadway production. This is the only instance in history that an Off-Broadway performance has done so.

 Brecht and Weill were originally hired to adapt the film, but Brecht quit halfway through the production and Weill was eventually fired. As mentioned before, capitalism rots!

Velvita

Chorizo Mac and Ché-ese

• • •

Inspired by €VITA

Music by Andrew Lloyd Webber*, Lyrics and Book by* Tim Rice

Opened on Broadway in 1979 at the Broadway Theatre

WE HAD TO LET IT HAPPEN, WE HAD TO MAKE MAC AND CHEESE. *Evita* follows the real-life story of Eva Perón née Eva Duarte, a poor girl from the province of Junín who grows up to be Madonna, um, we mean the first lady of Argentina. Though first lady is a tricky term, as some consider President Perón, her husband, a full-blown dictator. It's complicated. Loved and loathed, Evita proves to be a shrewd and expertly calculating woman who, although instrumental in consolidating power for her husband, never gets to become vice president as she ends up succumbing to cancer. And yes, this *is* a musical. And *this* is a mac and cheese inspired by that musical. To honor Patti LuPone's pipes (Broadway's original Evita), we use chorizo here to make this homey casserole even more robust. With almost two pounds of cheese (not actual Velveeta, but we couldn't resist the pun), nobody's going to cry for you when you serve this up at your next dinner party. You could serve a little salad on the side, just don't let it move to the center where it's not qualified. There's only one star to this dish and her name is Velvita.

1 pound elbow macaroni

Kosher salt

5 cups whole milk (don't use low-fat—it won't work)

2 tablespoons olive oil, plus more if necessary

1 pound raw Mexican chorizo, out of the casing (make sure it's RAW chorizo, not cooked Spanish chorizo)

1 red onion, minced

½ cup flour

4 cups shredded sharp cheddar cheese

2 cups shredded Monterey Jack cheese

1 cup panko breadcrumbs

2 tablespoons butter, melted

1. Heat the oven to 375°F. Spray a 9-by-13-inch baking dish with cooking spray.

2. Fill a pot with water, bring to a boil, and season with a few tablespoons of salt (it should taste like good broth). Add the macaroni and cook for 2 minutes less than the package directions. Drain, rinse under cold water to stop the cooking, drain again, and set aside.

3. In the same pot, warm the milk (don't let it boil). Set aside.

4. Meanwhile, in a large heavy-bottomed pot or Dutch oven, heat the olive oil on medium-high heat and add the chorizo, breaking up with a wooden spoon as it cooks. When it begins to brown, look at the bottom of the pan: If there's not a lot of fat that has rendered, add up to 2 tablespoons more of olive oil. (There should be a

RECIPE CONTINUES

slick of oil on the bottom of the pan to help make the roux later.) Add the onion, plus a pinch of salt, and cook until the onion softens. Add the flour and cook for 1 minute, stirring over medium heat.

5. Slowly add the warm milk, stirring thoroughly with each addition, until you have a smooth, creamy sauce that coats the back of a spoon. (It may need to perk away for a few minutes.) Off the heat, add 3 cups of the cheddar and 1½ cups of the Monterey Jack. Stir in the cooked macaroni.

6. Pour the mixture into the prepared pan, top with the remaining cheeses and sprinkle with the breadcrumbs. Drizzle with the melted butter and bake on a foil-lined baking sheet (in case any spills over) until brown on top, about 30 minutes. If the top doesn't brown to your liking, you can place it under the broiler; just keep a close eye on it. Let cool for 5 minutes, then serve.

COOKING NOTES

 If you want to make this ahead, put everything (minus the breadcrumbs and butter) together the night before you're ready to serve it. Top with the cheese, cover with foil, refrigerate, and when ready to bake, sprinkle with the breadcrumbs and the butter and cook for a few minutes longer under Perón's latest flame.

 If you can't find raw Mexican chorizo, you can substitute an equal amount of Italian sausage. As someone said to Evita when she went to Italy: "I'm still called an admiral, yet I gave up the sea long ago." (Not our best work, or Tim Rice's.)

LISTENING NOTES

 The iconic V-shaped arm position that Patti LuPone assumes in "Don't Cry for Me Argentina" was demonstrated to Patti one night by Eva Perón's ghost . . . purports Patti.

 Though generally not well received by critics, the Broadway musical took home seven Tony Awards in 1980, which goes to show when there's a Patti LuPone, there's a way.

 One of this book's authors loved the film adaptation so much as a kid, it was the first DVD he ever purchased. Can you guess which one? His name rhymes with Shmideon Shmick. Another author of this book loved the film adaptation so much as a kid, he saw it in theaters four times. Can you guess which one? His name rhymes with Madame Goberts.

Cats-erole

Tuna Casserole with Frizzabella Onions

• • •

Inspired by CATS

Music by Andrew Lloyd Webber, *Lyrics by* T. S. Eliot, Trevor Nunn
and Richard Stilgoe

Opened on Broadway in 1982 at the Winter Garden Theatre

THERE'S A WHISPER DOWN THE LINE, AT 11:39, THAT THERE'S tuna on your plate. Based on T. S. Eliot's 1939 collection of poetry, *Old Possum's Book of Practical Cats*, *Cats* is a musical about, well, cats. They all have names and personalities and are all eager to introduce themselves as they wriggle around the stage. There's a bit of a plot about the Jellicle Ball and who will be selected to go to the Heaviside Layer, but you really shouldn't worry about that. Nobody else has. And if you're worried about people's reactions when you say, "Tuna casserole," don't! This tuna casserole will rum tum tug at their taste buds. Using rotini pasta, which catches all the goodness on the twists and turns (think of it as a cat toy), this dish is freshened up with parsley and dill, and then made decadent and crispy with French's fried onions (aka frizzabella-d onions). One bite and you'll be floating up, up, up on a tire of your own happiness. Don't blame us if the tire has a hard time lifting off.

RECIPE CONTINUES

MAKES ONE 9-BY-13-INCH TUNA CASSEROLE

1 stick (½ cup) unsalted butter, plus more for greasing the pan

Kosher salt

One 16-ounce package rotini pasta (or any pasta of your choice)

½ cup all-purpose flour

4 cups whole milk, room temperature

1 tablespoon Dijon mustard

1 teaspoon kosher salt

½ teaspoon freshly ground black pepper

¼ teaspoon cayenne pepper

2 cans (5 ounces each) oil-packed tuna, flaked with a fork

2 cups shredded sharp white cheddar cheese

½ cup Parmesan

2 cups (10 ounces) frozen peas, no need to thaw

¼ cup chopped fresh parsley

¼ cup chopped fresh dill

Zest of 1 lemon

6 ounces French's fried onions

1. Grease a 9-by-13-inch pan with some softened butter (about a tablespoon). Preheat the oven to 375°F.

2. Bring water to a boil in a Dutch oven and season with a few tablespoons of salt so that it tastes like good broth (not the ocean). Add your pasta and cook for 2 minutes less than the package directions. Carefully drain and set aside.

3. In the same (now dry) Dutch oven, melt the stick of butter over medium-high heat and add the flour. Stir with a wooden spoon and cook the mixture for 1 minute to get rid of the floury taste. Slowly whisk in the milk and cook until the mixture is nice and thick and coats the back of a spoon, about 2 minutes.

4. Off the heat, stir in the Dijon mustard, salt, pepper, cayenne, tuna, half of the cheddar, half of the Parmesan, frozen peas, parsley, dill, and the lemon zest. (Taste here to adjust for salt and pepper.) Stir in the cooked pasta and pour into the prepared pan. Top with the remaining cheddar and Parmesan, and sprinkle the fried onions on top.

5. Bake for 20 to 25 minutes, until bubbling and golden brown. Allow to cool for 5 minutes before serving.

═══ COOKING NOTES ═══

 Bustopher Jones wouldn't stop with fried onions. Take this cats-erole one step further and use crushed-up potato chips on top! Bonus points for sour cream & onion, salt & vinegar, or Fancy Feast tender beef.

 Hate tuna? Not very feline of you, but that's okay. Just leave it out! Also skip the Dijon, dill, and lemon zest (they were there to enhance the tuna) and you're good to go.

LISTENING NOTES

 Investors scoffed at the idea of creating a musical about cats (if you can believe it), so Andrew Lloyd Webber ended up taking out a second mortgage on his home to initially finance the show. Smart move, Webber— that investment yielded a lot of cheese.

 Did you know that the original production of *Cats* used more than 3,000 pounds of yak hair for its wigs? That's a serious hairball.

 Marlene Danielle remained with the cast throughout its 18-year, record-breaking run, which is essentially the lifespan of a cat. Coincidence? We think so.

Crabaret

Crab Cakes with Two-Ladles-of-Garlic Aioli

• • •

Inspired by CABARET

Music by John Kander, *Lyrics by* Fred Ebb, *Book by* Joe Masteroff

Opened on Broadway in 1966 at the Broadhurst Theatre

WILLKOMMEN, BIENVENUE, WELCOME, ZU CRAB CAKES, AU crab cakes, to crab cakes! Based on John Van Druten's 1951 play, *I Am a Camera*, which in turn was adapted from Charles Isherwood's 1939 autobiographical novel, *Goodbye to Berlin*, *Cabaret* tells the story of American writer Cliff Bradshaw and his relationship with English cabaret performer—and honestly, absolute icon—Sally Bowles during the decline of the Weimar Republic in Berlin. Framed by the sinister and mischievous emcee named . . . the Emcee (also absolutely iconic), *Cabaret* still shocks, moves, and sets the audience ablaze with its heartrending torch songs and well, hate to break it you again, iconic musical numbers. How perfect, then, that we're sharing the recipe for these iconic crab cakes that comes to us from one of our own iconic fathers-in-law (Adam's!), Steve Johnson, of Bellingham, Washington. They're indisputably the world's best crab cakes (adapted from the *San Juan Classics Cookbook*), and although we wanted to give them some German flair, we just couldn't corrupt them. Eat them alone in a room or where the music plays; either way, we guarantee they couldn't please you more.

FOR THE GARLIC AIOLI

1½ cups mayonnaise
2 garlic cloves, grated
½ cup lemon juice
Pinch of salt

FOR THE CRAB CAKES

¼ cup mayonnaise
1 egg, beaten

½ cup panko bread-
    crumbs, plus more
    for breading
1 tablespoon all-purpose
    flour
2½ teaspoons fresh
    lemon juice
¼ cup finely diced red
    onion
½ teaspoon salt, plus
    more for sprinkling

¼ teaspoon freshly
    ground black pepper
4 cups (1 pound) fresh
    crabmeat, drained
    and squeezed dry
    over a colander in
    the sink
½ cup vegetable oil
Lemon wedges

TO MAKE THE GARLIC AIOLI

1. Whisk together the mayonnaise, garlic, lemon, and salt. Taste and adjust with more lemon and salt, as necessary.

TO MAKE THE CRAB CAKES

1. Preheat the oven to 250°F. Whisk together the mayonnaise, egg, breadcrumbs, flour, lemon juice, onion, salt, and pepper in a large bowl. Add the crabmeat, flaking it apart slightly as you do to feel for any shell (but try to keep big lumps of crab in there, too). Aggressively mix together with your hands and forcefully form 12 balls and flatten

RECIPE CONTINUES

them into patties. Fill a pie plate with more breadcrumbs (about a cup), season with a bit more salt, then press the patties into the breadcrumbs, coating on all sides.

2. Place a wire rack on a foil-lined tray. In a large nonstick skillet, heat the oil until shimmering but not smoking (350°F on a thermometer). Carefully place six of the crab cakes in the skillet and allow them to brown for 1 to 2 minutes on the first side, carefully flipping them over with a fish spatula to brown on the other. When finished, lift onto the baking sheet and keep warm in the oven while frying the remaining crab cakes.

3. Place the crab cakes on a platter with lemon wedges and serve with the garlic aioli on the side.

COOKING NOTES

 Maybe this time you'll get lucky and get to make these with fresh Dungeness crab from the Pacific Northwest. (If you're from Baltimore, please don't throw a brick through our window.) The fresher your crab, the better these will taste.

 Though the garlic aioli in this recipe is a perfectly marvelous shortcut, if you want to make the real thing, you can do that quickly with a blender, adapting a recipe from Ferran Adrià. Simply blend together 2 whole garlic cloves and 2 whole eggs. While the blender is whirring, slowly pour in 1¼ cups olive oil in a steady stream until an emulsion forms. Season it with salt and/or lemon juice and tomorrow will belong to you.

LISTENING NOTES

 Did you know that the song "I Don't Care Much" was written hastily at a dinner party? One night, Kander and Ebb found themselves bragging about their writing speed and Ebb boasted, "Clear the table, and we'll write you a song between dessert and coffee." When the writing duo went to the piano, Ebb asked Kander what they should write about and Kander responded, "I don't know. I don't care much." Ebb set it to a waltz and the rest is musical theater history.

 Cabaret was so successful that once Kander got a letter from a Jewish sleep-over camp asking if they could use "Tomorrow Belongs to Me" as a camp song. Confused, Kander wrote back and explained what the song was about . . .

 By 1966, Harold Prince had already made a name for himself as a director (and definitely as a producer), but *Cabaret* was his first financial directing success. The production ran for 1,665 performances, and his 1987 revival ran for 2,377.

The Clam's Visit

Clams from Papi's Ocean with Preserved Lemons on Israeli Couscous

• • •

Inspired by **THE BAND'S VISIT**

Music and Lyrics by David Yazbek, *Book by* Itamar Moses

Opened on Broadway in 2017 at the Ethel Barrymore Theatre

WHERE ARE YOU, WHERE ARE YOU, WILL THESE CLAMS ANSWER ME? Based on the 2007 Israeli film of the same name, *The Band's Visit* takes place in a remote Israeli desert town called Bet Hatikvah—with a *B*, not a *P*—when an Egyptian band arrives thinking they've come to Pet Hatikvah—with a *P*, not a *B*—and stays over for 24 hours until they can get on a bus outta there. Egyptians and Israelis connect, some canoodle, some cry, someone answers a phone, and ultimately our humanity is restored by the universality of longing and connection. Now let us connect your stomach with this clam and Israeli couscous dish. Think of this as a fantasy trip to the ocean (like Papi's): The couscous stands in for the wet sand and everything is bright and colorful with cherry tomatoes, preserved lemons, and cilantro. The key here is monitoring the liquid in the pan. Once the couscous is added, it will begin to absorb the liquid; you'll want to supplement with more water as necessary so there's still a bit of a sauce. The result should be a brothy, beachy treat, worthy of Umm Kulthum and Omar Sharif.

RECIPE CONTINUES

¼ cup olive oil, plus more for drizzling

1 small yellow onion, chopped (about 2 cups)

2 small fennel bulbs, cored and chopped (about 2 cups)

Kosher salt

5 garlic cloves, thinly sliced

1 bunch cilantro, stems thinly sliced, leaves roughly chopped and reserved for later

1 tablespoon cumin seeds

1 tablespoon harissa paste

3 cups cherry tomatoes (try to find multicolored heirloom cherry tomatoes, if you can)

1 cup dry white wine

2 cups Israeli couscous or M'hamsa hand-rolled couscous (see Cooking Notes)

3 cups water

1 preserved lemon, quartered, flesh removed, chopped

24 clams, rinsed (we like Manila or littlenecks)

Aleppo pepper

1. Heat the olive oil in a very large skillet or Dutch oven that has a lid over medium-high heat. Add the onion, fennel, and a pinch of salt and sauté for 8 to 10 minutes until starting to turn golden brown.

2. Add the garlic, cilantro stems (they have lots of flavor, too!), and cumin seeds and cook for 1 minute, being careful that the garlic doesn't burn—lowering the heat if necessary.

3. Stir in the harissa paste, coating everything, then add the cherry tomatoes and another pinch of salt. Cook for 1 minute, stirring to coat the tomatoes with everything else in the skillet. Add the wine and cook on high heat until most of the liquid evaporates, the tomatoes begin to burst open, and everything begins to look saucy, about 10 minutes.

4. Add the couscous and water, stir all around, and bring to a boil. Lower to a gentle simmer and partially cover with a lid. Cook until most of the liquid is absorbed, but the mixture is still slightly wet, 3 to 5 minutes.

5. Stir in the preserved lemon and then nestle the clams on top of the couscous. Put the lid back on and cook on high heat for 2 minutes until the clams open. Turn off the heat, lift out the opened clams onto a plate (discard any that don't open), stir the couscous, and taste. Adjust for salt (it can take up to another teaspoon).

6. To serve, spoon the couscous mixture into bowls, top with some clams, drizzle with olive oil, sprinkle with Aleppo pepper, and garnish with the cilantro leaves.

COOKING NOTES

 To honor the specificity of *The Band's Visit*, here are some specific brands that we recommend using for this recipe. For the couscous, we like M'hamsa, which is neither Israeli nor Egyptian (it comes from Tunisia), but has a rugged, toasted quality that's far more interesting than the more uniformly pearled Israeli couscous. For the harissa paste, we like Entube— which comes in an actual tube, so you can save the rest in the fridge for another use (just be very careful to not confuse it with your toothpaste). And, finally, for the preserved lemon, we like the Les Moulins brand.

 If you're looking for something different, try making this recipe with shrimp instead of clams. At the step where you nuzzle in the clams, nuzzle in the shrimp, and cook with the lid on until the shrimp turn pink. Although it may be hard to find shrimp in the middle of nowhere.

LISTENING NOTES

 Did you know that legendary director and producer Hal Prince (the director of *ahem* the original *Cabaret*, *Sweeney Todd*, *Evita*, *The Phantom of the Opera*, and many more) was originally attached to the project? He shaped and developed it for years before David Cromer took on the piece. The show originally took place in Germany, where a barber was making meat pies out of enemies, all guided by a Machiavellian woman in a mask. JK.

 The creators have spoken about how they were attracted to the piece because of its "unspectacular"-ness. The show is sort of an anti-musical. Its beauty comes from its stillness, which you can hear throughout its klezmer-based score.

 As of *Swiss Chards'* publication, *The Band's Visit* is currently tied in third place for musicals with most Tony Award wins (10) with *Hello, Dolly!*, *Billy Elliot*, and *Moulin Rouge!*. They are behind *Hamilton* (11) and *The Producers* (12). That unspectacular-ness yielded some spectacular results.

Codspell

Poached Cod with Mussels and All Good Gifts

• • •

Inspired by GODSPELL

Music and Lyrics by Stephen Schwartz *and Book by* John-Michael Tebelak

Opened on Broadway in 1976 at the Broadhurst Theatre

P REPARE YE, THE FISH IN A BOWL. BASED ON A LITTLE BOOK called the Bible, *Godspell* brings us fully grown adults dressed as hippie clowns who recite parables, most specifically from the Gospel of Matthew, and sing hymns set to Stephen Schwartz music. (Finally, a good Jewish boy's interpretation of the New Testament.) Throughout the show, Jesus teaches our young hippies biblical life lessons, but this light show *really* takes a dark turn at the end . . . when Jesus gets crucified. So let's brighten things up with a summery cod dish that uses beautiful heirloom tomatoes and basil from the farmers' market. If you can't get to a farmers' market, we beseech thee: Make this with the best tomatoes you can find. If tomatoes aren't in season, you *could* make this with canned tomatoes, but we can't guarantee that you'll be blessed.

3 tablespoons extra-virgin
olive oil, plus more for
drizzling

4 fat garlic cloves, thinly
sliced

Pinch red pepper flakes

1 cup dry white wine
(something you like to
drink)

3 large heirloom
tomatoes (various
colors), cored and
roughly chopped

2 cups sun gold tomatoes
or small cherry
tomatoes

Kosher salt

1 cup fresh basil,
shredded

2 fillets cod, about
4 ounces each

Freshly ground black
pepper

12 mussels, debearded
and rinsed

Grilled bread, for serving

1. First, make the sauce/poaching liquid. In a large sauté pan with a lid, heat the olive
   oil and garlic until the garlic starts to take on a little color. Add a pinch of red pepper
   flakes, then the wine—it will sizzle and spatter, that's okay.

2. Bring the wine to a boil, then add all the heirloom tomatoes and sun gold tomatoes,
   plus a teaspoon of kosher salt. Add half of the basil, bring to a boil again and cook,
   covered, until the tomatoes begin to break down and thicken, about 5 minutes.

RECIPE CONTINUES

3. Season the fish on both sides with more salt and pepper, then lower into the poaching liquid. Surround the fish with the mussels and place the lid on the pan, over medium-high heat.

4. Cook for 3 minutes, then lift the lid and check to see if the mussels are open. As soon as they open, remove them to a bowl. Cover and continue cooking the fish a few minutes more until a thermometer reads 125°F when inserted into the center.

5. To serve, lift the cod into shallow bowls, surround with some of the mussels, spoon the sauce over, plus a sprinkling of the remaining shredded basil. Drizzle with more olive oil and serve with the grilled bread.

=== COOKING NOTES ===

 Can't find cod? It's all for the best: Just use halibut instead (or any other firm white fish).

 If the mussels don't open after cooking, turn back, oh man! You'll want to throw those mussels away (they're probably bad).

LISTENING NOTES

 Did you know that the 1972 Toronto company of *Godspell* started the careers of Gilda Radner, Eugene Levy, Andrea Martin, Victor Garber, and Martin Short? They were all in the same production with music director Paul Shaffer. Oh, Canada.

 The original version of *Godspell* was actually book writer John-Michael Tebelak's thesis project at Carnegie Mellon. Schwartz only came on later when the show made its way to that beautiful city—NYC.

 "Day by Day," *Godspell*'s most well-known song, has been referenced time and again in pop culture. In *Meet the Parents*, Ben Stiller's character recites the lines to the song when asked to say grace. In *Wet Hot American Summer*, the song is performed at a camp talent show. And Christian rock band DC Talk cover it on their album *Jesus Freak*.

Spring A-wok-ening

Stir-Fried Spring Vegetables
with Totally Plucked Chicken

• • •

Inspired by SPRING AWAKENING

Music by Duncan Sheik, *Book and Lyrics by* Steven Sater

Opened on Broadway in 2006 at the Eugene O'Neill Theatre

CHICKEN STIR FRY, EVERY OTHER DAY. *SPRING AWAKENING* reimagines the 1891 Frank Wedekind play of the same name as a rock musical where 19th-century German schoolchildren in breeches take out microphones and sing out their feelings. And sometimes touch themselves. The show centers around the rebellious Melchior, the fatally curious Wendla, and the sad sleepyhead Moritz, and explores subjects like premarital sex, masturbation, homosexuality, incest, suicide, abortions, and *really* strict adults. If you're strict about your diet, here's a healthy springy stir-fry that's not at all a bitch to make. Just do a quick marinade for your chicken thighs, sear them in a hot wok (or skillet), add your aromatics (ginger and garlic), your spring vegetables (asparagus and sugar snap peas, but feel free to try other spring favorites like peas or radishes), and finally the other half of the marinade for a delectable dinner that still leaves you time to do your 80 lines of Virgil, 16 equations, and a paper on the Habsburgs.

RECIPE CONTINUES

¼ cup low-sodium soy sauce

¼ cup fish sauce

¼ cup honey

1 tablespoon sriracha

3 tablespoons toasted sesame oil

3 tablespoons rice wine vinegar

1¼ pounds boneless, skinless chicken thighs, cut into 1-inch strips

4 tablespoons grapeseed oil or other neutral oil

2 tablespoons peeled and chopped fresh ginger

3 fat garlic cloves, minced

1 pound asparagus, thick bottoms removed, sliced into ½-inch pieces on the extreme bias

1 pound sugar snap peas, stemmed, sliced in half on the extreme bias

Cooked rice, for serving

White sesame seeds, for garnish

1. Whisk together the soy sauce, fish sauce, honey, sriracha, toasted sesame oil, and rice wine vinegar and divide into two bowls. Add the boneless, skinless chicken thighs to the first bowl and marinate at room temperature for 15 minutes.

2. Heat a large, seasoned wok (or, if you don't have a wok, a very large metal skillet) on high heat for 2 minutes. Meanwhile, remove the chicken thighs from the marinade (discard the liquid) and pat them very dry with paper towels. Swirl 2 tablespoons of the grapeseed oil into the hot wok (it should smoke) and carefully lay in the chicken. Sear all over, stirring with a metal spatula, until golden brown on the outside and

cooked all the way through, 3 to 4 minutes. (If the chicken gives off a lot of liquid, and it might, wait for that liquid to boil off with the chicken still in the pan, and then it should begin to sizzle and brown.) Remove the chicken to a plate.

3. Swirl in the remaining grapeseed oil and add the ginger and garlic. Stir around, then quickly add the asparagus and sugar snap peas, stirring all around, until the vegetables take on color and a knife goes through the asparagus easily, 3 to 4 minutes.

4. Return the chicken to the pan and pour in the second bowl from the first step. Stir all around and cook until everything is coated and the liquid has thickened slightly, about 2 minutes. Serve over rice with sesame seeds to garnish.

COOKING NOTES

 As the seasons change, so can the vegetables in your stir-fry. For a song of purple summer, try zucchini and fresh corn cut straight off the cob. When autumn and wind always want to creep up and haunt you, try Brussels sprouts and squash. And in winter walking after a storm, go for mushrooms and broccoli.

 If your kids are so sick of chicken that they think this dish is totally f***ed, try switching up the protein. Shrimp will work great here and so will firm tofu—just pat it really dry first.

LISTENING NOTES

 Did you know that Lea Michele, the original Wendla, workshopped the show starting from the age of 14 for six years before the show made it to Broadway? By 20, Lea had successfully stuck with the show all the way up to its Broadway debut. She was not going to be left behind.

 In 2015, Deaf West staged a moving and beautiful Broadway revival of *Spring Awakening*. The show was performed simultaneously in English and American Sign Language with a cast of hearing and deaf actors. Krysta Rodriguez was actually in the original 2006 production *and* the revival. She should be grateful to the mama who bore her for those age-defying genes.

 Of the original cast members, 10 out of 17 made their Broadway debuts in this show, some of whom had to be tutored throughout the run of the show because of their age (one of *Swiss Chards'* authors, included). The show also marked the Broadway debut of its choreographer, who won a Tony Award for this show, the legendary modern dance pioneer, Bill T. Jones. Bill didn't have to be tutored, though.

Chicken Breast Side Story

Pineapple Maria-nated Chicken Breast with Fried Plantains and Sazón Rice

• • •

Inspired by WEST SIDE STORY

Music by Leonard Bernstein, *Lyrics by* Stephen Sondheim, *Book by* Arthur Laurents

Opened on Broadway in 1957 at the Winter Garden Theatre

THE MOST BEAUTIFUL SOUND YOU'VE EVER HEARD . . . CHICKEN breast. This groundbreaking musical sets William Shakespeare's *Romeo and Juliet* in 1950s NYC and tells the tragic love story of Maria and Tony against the backdrop of dueling street gangs, the Jets and the Sharks. If you ever thought street gangs couldn't snap and spin balletically while still being menacing, you might be right, but still, it was a great try, Jerome! With a Sharky nod to old San Juan, "island of tropical breezes" and "pineapples growing," and a Jets-inspired protein, the whitest white meat, a chicken breast, this is a marriage as potentially fraught as Tony and Maria's. But with the help of a citrusy marinate, Sazón rice, and some fried plantains, this dish has a happier ending than the musical it's based on.

FOR THE MARINADE

¼ cup olive oil

⅓ cup freshly squeezed
orange juice

⅓ cup freshly squeezed
lime juice

⅓ cup freshly squeezed
lemon juice

1 teaspoon kosher salt

1 teaspoon freshly
ground black pepper

1 teaspoon ground
coriander

1 teaspoon garlic powder

1 teaspoon dried oregano

1 teaspoon ground cumin

FOR THE SAZÓN RICE

2 tablespoons butter

1 onion, chopped

1 cup jasmine rice

1 Sazón packet (we
recommend Goya)

1 teaspoon kosher salt

2 cups water

FOR THE CHICKEN

4 boneless, skinless
chicken breasts

3 tablespoons vegetable
oil

FOR THE PLANTAINS

2 very ripe plantains
(they should be close
to black)

½ cup vegetable oil

Kosher salt

TO FINISH

Lime wedges

Chopped cilantro

RECIPE CONTINUES

TO MAKE THE MARINADE

1. Whisk together all the marinade ingredients and pour into a large freezer bag or plastic container. Add the chicken breasts, squish all around, and marinate for at least 2 and up to 4 hours in the refrigerator.

2. When ready to cook, take the chicken out of the fridge to come to room temperature and start by making the rice.

TO MAKE THE SAZÓN RICE

1. Rinse the rice in a sifter under cold water in the sink until the water runs clear.

2. In a large pot, heat the butter over high heat and, when foaming, add the onion and a pinch of salt. Lower the heat to medium and cook until the onion is translucent. Add the rice and toast, on medium heat, for a few minutes until the rice is well coated in the butter. Add the Sazón packet, salt, and water and bring to a boil. Lower to a gentle simmer (medium-low), cover, and cook for 12 to 15 minutes, until the liquid is absorbed and the rice is cooked through. Set aside, turn off the heat, let sit for 10 minutes, then fluff with a fork.

TO MAKE THE CHICKEN

1. Pat the chicken breasts very dry with paper towels and season with a bit more salt and pepper. Heat a large cast-iron skillet on high heat, add the oil, and sear the chicken without moving it for 3 minutes.

2. Flip to the other side and continue cooking until a thermometer registers 150°F when inserted into the center of the breast. Remove to a plate to rest, tented with foil.

TO MAKE THE PLANTAINS

1. Use a knife to cut off the ends of the plantains, peel them, and slice into 1-inch pieces on the bias. Heat the oil in the same skillet where you cooked the chicken until it sizzles when you lower a plantain into it.

2. Carefully fry the plantain pieces, a few at a time—because of all the sugar in them, they burn quickly—until golden brown all over, about 6 minutes, seasoning with salt when you remove them.

TO FINISH

1. Spoon rice onto each plate, top with a chicken breast, and place the plantains alongside. Drizzle with all the drippings from the resting chicken (a key step). Serve with lime wedges and more cilantro to garnish.

If you really want to get your kicks tonight, make this recipe with boneless, skinless chicken thighs instead of chicken breasts. The thighs take on more of the marinade, retain their moisture as they cook, and get charred in spots, making them sexy enough to start a rumble.

 Plantains begin like very starchy bananas and, as they ripen, they become sweeter. If your plantains aren't ripening fast enough, place them in a paper bag with an apple overnight. Soon they'll be as raring to go as Tony in Act One.

LISTENING NOTES

 Did you know that this was Stephen Sondheim's first musical? He only wrote the lyrics to this one and has famously said that his work on it was trite. Can you imagine thinking your work on one of the greatest musicals of all time was just . . . fine? We stan.

 The acclaimed director and choreographer of the original musical, Jerome Robbins, prohibited the actors playing the Jets and the Sharks to interact with each other off stage in hopes of fueling real feelings of divisiveness. Too bad he couldn't have just signed them up for Twitter.

 When working on *West Side Story*, Bernstein was doing double duty as he was simultaneously composing for *Candide* as well. In fact, he did a full duet swap between the two musicals. "One Hand, One Heart" was originally written for Candide and Cunégonde, and "O Happy We" was originally written for Tony and Maria. Who knew these characters were such swingers? We wonder what Anita would have to say about all of that.

Grease (Is the Bird)

Summer-Lovin' Fried Chicken with Hot Honey

• • •

Inspired by GREASE

Music, Lyrics, and Book by Jim Jacobs *and* Warren Casey

Opened on Broadway in 1972 at the Eden Theatre

LOOK AT ME I'M FRIED CHICKEN-Y, LOUSY WITH HOT, HOT HONEY. *Grease* follows saintly Sandy and greaser Danny who reconnect at Rydell High after a hot summer of love. Upon reunion, Danny behaves like a real toxic white cis-het tool in front of his T-Birds gang (originally Burger Palace Boys, see Listening Notes) and pretends to completely not know Sandy. But do not worry, with the help of the Pink Ladies, Sandy transforms herself from a goody two-shoes into a greaser fantasy and *really* wins over Danny, which only goes to show that the way to win a man's heart is to change everything about yourself! You won't want to change anything about this fried chicken, however. Soaked in hot-sauce-flavored buttermilk overnight to tenderize the meat, and then coated in a robust mixture of spices, this fried chicken is lightning right out of the skillet . . . but it gets even more supreme with hot honey drizzled all over the top. Everyone's going to want you to tell them more, tell them more about the recipe, but don't. Just tell them to buy this book.

3 cups buttermilk

10 dashes hot sauce (Tabasco or Crystal work great)

1 tablespoon kosher salt, plus more for later

4 chicken legs

4 chicken thighs

1 cup honey

1 red chili (Fresno or jalapeño), thinly sliced, seeds discarded

1 teaspoon red chili flakes

3 cups all-purpose flour

1 tablespoon smoked paprika

1 tablespoon garlic powder

1 teaspoon freshly ground black pepper

½ teaspoon cayenne pepper

Vegetable, canola, or peanut oil

1. The day before you want to fry the chicken, pour the buttermilk into a large container with a lid or a bowl and whisk in the 10 dashes of hot sauce and the tablespoon of salt. Add the chicken pieces, making sure all of them are thoroughly coated, put the lid on (or cover with plastic wrap), and refrigerate overnight.

RECIPE CONTINUES

2. An hour before you're ready to fry, take the chicken out of the refrigerator and allow it to come to room temperature. While that's happening, make your hot honey by combining the honey, chili, and the red chili flakes in a small saucepan. Heat on medium and, when it just starts to simmer, lower the heat to low, keeping an eye on it so it doesn't bubble up, and cook for 5 minutes. Pour into a bowl and set aside while you make your chicken.

3. Preheat the oven to 250°F.

4. In a large bowl, whisk together the flour, smoked paprika, garlic powder, black pepper, cayenne, and 1 tablespoon of salt. Remove each piece of chicken from the buttermilk, allow some of the liquid to drip off, and press it into the flour mixture. Be sure to really press the flour mixture into the chicken. The more you get on there, the crustier your chicken will be.

5. Fill a large cast-iron skillet one-third of the way with oil. Heat on medium-high and when the oil reaches 350°F on a thermometer, carefully lower your chicken into the oil. Be sure to go slowly—you don't want the oil to come up over the sides and start a grease fire. Best to work in batches. Cook your first batch, turning the chicken with tongs every few minutes, until the chicken is deep golden brown all over and an internal thermometer reads 165°F when inserted into the thickest piece, 10 to 12 minutes. Lift onto a baking sheet, sprinkle it with a little more salt, and keep warm in the oven. When the second batch is done, sprinkle again with a little salt, remove the first batch from the oven, and serve all the chicken on a platter with the hot honey on the side.

COOKING NOTES

You don't need a cast-iron skillet to make fried chicken. You can do it in a Dutch oven, for example, and deep-fry. But cast-iron skillets are cheap and, more important, they retain their heat so that your fried chicken will come out crispy and sexy enough to lower its sunglasses, look you in the eye, and say, "Tell me about it, stud."

The spices in the dredge are variable depending on your tastes. Like it spicier? Add more cayenne. Want more of an oniony flavor? Throw in some onion powder. Just make sure to choose spices that go together like *rama lama lama ka dinga da dinga dong*.

If the use of Burger Palace Boys threw you for a loop, you're not alone. That was the original moniker for the male Rydell gang in the first Broadway production. The 1978 film adaptation, however, changed the gang's name and, given the outrageous success of the film, all subsequent productions adopted the T-Birds instead.

 The original Roger in *Grease* was Broadway's own Walter Bobbie, who ended up switching careers and went on to direct the longest running Broadway revival of all time, *Chicago.* Better career move than being a beauty school dropout.

 Another notable performer in *Grease*'s original lineage emerged from its West-End debut—none other than Richard Gere. Gere played Danny Zuko in its 1973 London premiere. He was an understudy in the American production.

Hedwig and the Angry Sandwich

Pig-in-a-Box Pulled Pork Sliders

• • •

Inspired by HEDWIG AND THE ANGRY INCH

Music and Lyrics by Stephen Trask*, Book by* John Cameron Mitchell

Opened on Broadway in 2014 at the Belasco Theatre

MAKE ME SOME COLESLAW, AND HEAT UP SOME PORK BUTT, AND stick it on a bun. *Hedwig and the Angry Inch* is a rock musical told through the eyes of genderqueer rocker Hedwig Robinson neé Hansel Schmidt. Hedwig tells the audience her story of escaping East Berlin after being convinced by an American soldier to get reconstructive surgery to pose as a woman and marry him (you know, the American dream). Upon making it to America, Hedwig's husband leaves her for another man and, to survive, Hedwig becomes a babysitter. The brother of a kid she sits for takes a liking to Hedwig, Hedwig transforms him into a rock god, he abandons her, and ultimately, Hedwig decides to give the stage to her new husband, a Jewish drag queen (played by a woman), whom Hedwig had previously prohibited from acting as a woman in a jealous fit. Look, you had to be there. And everyone will want to be in your kitchen when you make this pulled pork sandwich with homemade BBQ sauce and sauerkraut-infused coleslaw (a nod to Hedwig's roots). This is the perfect thing to eat in your trailer park on nights when the world's a bit amiss. Be sure to save one for your sugar daddy.

FOR THE PORK

2 tablespoons kosher salt

3 tablespoons dark brown sugar

1 tablespoon chili powder

1 tablespoon smoked paprika

1 tablespoon ground coriander

1 tablespoon ground cumin

1 tablespoon cracked black pepper

¼ teaspoon cayenne pepper

1 tablespoon garlic powder

One 3-pound Boston butt pork roast

2 tablespoons vegetable oil

4 cups (32 ounces) German beer (we used Carlsberg)

FOR THE SAUCE

1½ cups ketchup

1 tablespoon Dijon mustard

1 tablespoon Worcestershire sauce

½ cup cider vinegar

½ cup dark brown sugar

1½ teaspoons salt

½ teaspoon black pepper

FOR THE SLAW

1 small green cabbage, shredded

1 red onion, thinly sliced

2 carrots, shredded

1 bunch scallions, sliced thin

½ cup chopped Italian parsley

1 cup prepared sauerkraut

½ cup mayonnaise

1 tablespoon Dijon mustard

1 tablespoon cider vinegar

1 teaspoon kosher salt

TO SERVE

8 to 12 slider buns

RECIPE CONTINUES

TO MAKE THE PORK

1. Preheat the oven to 300°F.

2. Combine the salt, brown sugar, chili powder, smoked paprika, coriander, cumin, black pepper, cayenne pepper, and garlic powder. Pat the pork butt dry and then rub all over with the spice mix. (You can do this ahead, and the pork will be even more flavorful: up to 24 hours in the refrigerator.)

3. In a Dutch oven large enough to hold the pork butt with the lid on, heat the oil until very hot. Sear the pork butt, being careful not to let it burn (the sugar will make it burn faster), until golden brown all over. Lift the pork out of the pan onto a plate, turn off the heat, and using wads of paper towels, wipe out any burnt sugar at the bottom of the pan (this will ruin the flavor later on). You don't have to be too meticulous, just get out anything that's burnt.

4. Pour in the beer, bring to a boil, and use a wooden spoon to dislodge any brown bits from the bottom of the pan. Place the pork back in, put the lid on, and place in the oven for 3 hours, rotating the pork butt every hour or so.

TO MAKE THE SAUCE

1. Make the sauce by combining the ketchup, mustard, Worcestershire, cider vinegar, brown sugar, salt, and pepper in a medium saucepan and simmer for 5 minutes. Set aside.

TO MAKE THE SLAW

1. Make the slaw by combining the cabbage, onion, carrots, scallions, parsley, sauerkraut, mayonnaise, mustard, cider vinegar, and salt in a large bowl. Taste and adjust for vinegar and salt—it should be punchy and bright.

TO SERVE

1. After 3 hours, carefully remove the lid on the pork and cook for another 30 minutes, flipping halfway through, until the outside of the pork is nicely bronzed, the meat pulls apart easily, and a thermometer reads 200°F.

2. Allow the meat to rest for a few minutes, then shred with two forks, discarding any fat that looks unappetizing.

3. Assemble the sliders by piling on the shredded meat, some of the sauce, and some of the slaw. Serve with a 1-inch pickle.

If you, like Hedwig, want something a bit stiffer than beer in your braise, turn off the heat and add ¼ cup bourbon, turn on the heat to work up the brown bits, then add 4 cups of chicken stock and proceed.

 If Tommy Gnosis is coming over for dinner and you want to make this a bit fancier, do away with the buns, the slaw, and the sauce, and instead of shredding the pork, slice it against the grain and serve over polenta with some of the pan juices.

 Despite being an Off-Broadway sensation in 1998 and a film in 2001, both starring its co-creator, John Cameron Mitchell, *Hedwig and the Angry Inch* didn't actually make it to Broadway until 2014, where it starred Neil Patrick Harris.

 The music of *Hedwig* is greatly influenced by the punk music of Iggy Pop, Lou Reed, and the 1970s glam rock of David Bowie, who actually was so taken with the musical that he co-produced its LA production. He (origin of) love(d) it.

 The creators of *Hedwig*, Stephen Trask and John Cameron Mitchell, met on an LA–NYC flight in 1989. They were drawn to each other by a "common aesthetic," according to Trask, as they were the only ones on the plane not watching *When Harry Met Sally. . . . When John Met Stephen . . .* is more like it!

Sunday in the Pork with George

Color-and-Light Pork Meatballs in Tomato Sauce

• • •

Inspired by SUNDAY IN THE PARK WITH GEORGE
Music and Lyrics by Stephen Sondheim, *Book by* James Lapine
Opened on Broadway in 1984 at the Booth Theatre

ORDER, DESIGN, TENSION, COMPOSITION, BALANCE, LIGHT, meatballs. *Sunday in the Park with George* is the groundbreaking musical about Pointillist painter, Georges Seurat, and the creation of his master-piece, *Sunday Afternoon on the Island of La Grande Jatte*. The show's got everything: Pointillism humor (George's love interest is named Dot; get it?), dog impressions, and the greatest romantic love song ever sung between a great-grandmother and her great-grandson (we've all been there). You'll feel just like Seurat when you make these meatballs, which are dotted with flecks of color and light by way of onions, carrots, and multicolored peppers. When you're done cooking, you'll look down at your red red red red red red orange red red orange dinner and say: "Look I made a meatball . . . where there never was a meatball."

One 28-ounce can whole San Marzano tomatoes

1 medium red onion, roughly chopped

1 red pepper, roughly chopped

1 yellow pepper, roughly chopped

1 carrot, peeled, roughly chopped

1 stalk of celery, roughly chopped

4 garlic cloves, smashed and peeled

½ cup extra-virgin olive oil, plus more for frying meatballs

Kosher salt

Freshly ground black pepper

1 pound ground pork

1 egg, slightly beaten

⅓ cup panko breadcrumbs

¼ cup freshly grated Parmesan cheese, plus more for sprinkling

¼ cup finely chopped Italian parsley, plus more for sprinkling

Pinch red chili flakes

1. Pour the tomatoes into a large bowl and crush them by hand. Fill the tomato can one-quarter of the way with water, swish around, and add to the bowl with the tomatoes.

2. Place the roughly chopped onion, red and yellow peppers, carrot, celery, and garlic in the bowl of a food processor. Pulse until the mixture is broken down but not completely liquid; it should look like vegetable confetti.

RECIPE CONTINUES

3. Heat a large metal skillet over medium-high heat. Pour in the olive oil, then add the vegetables, plus 1 teaspoon each of salt and black pepper. Stir until the liquid starts to release. (It should sizzle.) Lower the heat to medium, continue cooking and stirring, until all the moisture evaporates, up to 10 minutes. When the bottom of the pan is mostly dry again, allow the vegetables to cook a bit more until very lightly golden. Place half of the mixture in one small bowl and the other half in a larger bowl. Allow to cool completely. (You can use the freezer to speed things up.)

4. To the larger bowl with the other half of the vegetables, add the ground pork, egg, breadcrumbs, Parmesan, parsley, red chili flakes, plus another teaspoon of salt and ½ teaspoon of pepper.

5. Mix the ground pork mixture loosely by hand until everything is well distributed. Using a ¼-cup ice cream scoop with a lever, scoop balls of meat, shape lightly with your hands, and place on a baking sheet.

6. Wipe out the skillet with paper towels and pour in another ¼ cup of olive oil. Heat the oil on medium high heat until very hot. Working a few meatballs at a time (so you don't crowd the pan), brown the meatballs on all sides. You're not cooking the meatballs through here—just getting color. Set the meatballs aside once brown and continue browning the rest.

7. When all the meatballs are brown and set aside, pour out the oil and carefully wipe out any black bits with paper towels. Lower the heat in the skillet and pour in the sautéed vegetable mixture that you set aside earlier. (Remember that first bowl?) Raise the heat to medium until the vegetables are sizzling, then add the tomatoes and another teaspoon of salt, stirring everything together.

8. When the tomato mixture is at a simmer, return the meatballs to the skillet. Allow to cook on medium-high heat, uncovered, rotating the meatballs occasionally until they reach an internal temperature of 165°F. Once they reach that temperature, remove them to a plate and continue cooking the sauce until thickened nicely. (It should have the consistency of oatmeal.)

9. To serve, place the meatballs on a plate, top with the sauce, a drizzle of olive oil, more parsley, and more Parmesan. Serve with crusty bread and a small salad.

White: a blank page or canvas. Well that is until you splatter meatball juice all over it! A neater way to brown the meatballs in step 6 is to broil them in the oven. Simply place them on a foil-lined baking sheet sprayed with cooking spray, place a few inches under the broiler, and monitor them. As they brown on one side, rotate them all around until they're brown all over. Then add to the sauce in step 8.

 If you want to know if your meat is properly seasoned, make a test meatball by frying a small piece of the seasoned meat in a little olive oil before shaping the rest of the meatballs. Then you'll know for sure if it's got balance, light, and harmony.

 Did you know that when *Sunday* first premiered Off-Broadway, it was only one act? They only started performing the second act on the last three performances of its run.

 "Finishing the Hat" depicts exactly what it's like to get so absorbed in your creative work that the entire world falls away, so definitely listen to that while making the meatballs. And "Move On" will for sure make you weep (if not, you're a monster) so be sure to save that song for when chopping up the onions and kill two birds with one stone.

 Bernadette Peters didn't initially agree to the Broadway transfer of *Sunday* because she didn't feel she had a moment like Seurat did with "Finishing the Hat." Sondheim's response? "We Do Not Belong Together"—one of the most haunting love songs in the canon! Maybe "Lesson #8" was really listen to Bernadette.

She Loafs Me

Will He Like Me-atloaf with Vanilla Bean Mashed Sweet Potatoes

• • •

Inspired by SHE LOVES ME

Music by Jerry Bock, *Lyrics by* Sheldon Harnick, *and Book by* Joe Masteroff

Opened on Broadway in 1963 at the Eugene O'Neill Theatre

MEATLOAF, WE'RE MAKING MEATLOAF, IMAGINE THAT. BASED ON the 1937 play, *Parfumerie,* by Miklós László, which was also adapted into three, count 'em, three different films—1940's *The Shop Around the Corner*, 1949's *In the Good Old Summertime*, and 1998's *You've Got Mail, She Loves Me* (a clearly enduring story) follows Amalia Balash and Georg Nowack, coworkers at a parfumerie who absolutely loathe each other and are unknowingly writing each other love letters. They're enemies on the streets, but lovers on the sheets . . . of paper. After two acts of glorious dancing and glorious singing, Amalia and Georg realize it was love all along, and live happily ever after (or so we presume). And you will live happily ever after after making this meatloaf (or so we presume). The recipe is an easy sell: applewood smoked bacon, chilis in adobo, and lots of spices make this meatloaf the perfect pairing for vanilla bean mashed sweet potatoes, a nod to the most famous song in the show ("Vanilla Ice Cream"); the sweetness helps temper the intensity of the spicy meat. This makes enough to feed an entire department store—well, at least four hungry people—so prepare to have some leftovers. Give them to a dear friend.

FOR THE VANILLA BEAN MASHED SWEET POTATOES

4 large sweet potatoes, about 3 pounds

½ cup heavy cream

2 teaspoons vanilla bean paste (we like Heilala)

4 tablespoons butter, cubed

1 tablespoon kosher salt

FOR THE MEATLOAF

1 cup panko breadcrumbs

¼ cup whole milk

4 slices applewood smoked bacon (we like Nueske's), snipped with scissors into ¼-inch pieces

1 red onion, peeled and roughly chopped

1 carrot, top cut off, peeled and roughly chopped

1 celery stalk, roughly chopped

6 large garlic cloves, smashed and peeled

½ cup cilantro leaves, a few leaves reserved for garnish

1 pound ground pork

1 pound ground beef (20% fat, if possible)

3 large eggs, lightly beaten

2 teaspoons kosher salt

1 teaspoon freshly ground black pepper

1 teaspoon ground cumin

1 teaspoon chili powder

1 teaspoon smoked paprika

¼ teaspoon cayenne pepper

1 cup ketchup

2 chilis in adobo (use more if you like it very spicy)

1 tablespoon dark brown sugar

RECIPE CONTINUES

TO PREPARE THE MASHED SWEET POTATOES

1. Preheat the oven to 350°F and place the racks with enough space between them for you to both bake the sweet potatoes and cook the meatloaf.

2. Place the sweet potatoes on a foil-lined baking sheet, prick them all over with a fork, and bake for 60 to 90 minutes (depending on the size of the potatoes), until a knife goes through all of them without any resistance. Set them aside to cool.

TO MAKE THE MEATLOAF

1. While the sweet potatoes are roasting, make the meatloaf. In a large bowl, combine the breadcrumbs and milk and set aside for at least 5 minutes.

2. In a food processor, combine the bacon, onion, carrot, celery, garlic, and cilantro. Blend until it looks like a paste, 15 to 30 seconds.

3. Scrape the paste into the bowl with the breadcrumbs and add the pork, beef, eggs, salt, pepper, cumin, chili powder, smoked paprika, and cayenne pepper. Combine everything together with your hands, trying to create a homogenous mixture without compacting things too much (the meatloaf will be lighter the less you work it).

4. Spray a 9-inch loaf pan with cooking spray and press in the meatloaf, mounding it at the top into an arc. Place on a foil-lined tray (because of the fat, it will leak) and bake for 1 hour.

5. Clean the food processor and blend together the ketchup, the chilis in adobo, and the brown sugar for 30 seconds. When the meatloaf has been in the oven for 1 hour, brush the top generously with the adobo ketchup mixture (any left over can be served with the meatloaf) and bake for another 15 to 30 minutes, or until a thermometer reads 160°F all throughout and the top is nicely glazed. Let it rest for 10 minutes.

TO MAKE THE VANILLA BEAN MASHED SWEET POTATOES

1. Clean the food processor again. Peel the sweet potatoes with a small knife and place in the food processor.

2. Pour the cream into a small pot with the vanilla bean paste and heat until the cream is just bubbling around the edges.

3. Pour over the sweet potatoes and pulse a few times. Add the cubed butter and salt and blend for 3 to 5 minutes, until everything is nicely creamy. Taste and adjust for seasoning.

4. To serve, run a knife around the meatloaf and carefully flip it out onto a plate (juices may run out, so be careful), then flip it back upright. Slice into 1-inch slices and serve over the mashed sweet potatoes, garnishing with a few cilantro leaves.

COOKING NOTES

 If you want a leaner meatloaf for your date tonight at 8, try free-forming it directly on the foil-lined baking sheet. This has three advantages: (1) You can get the glaze all over the meatloaf; (2) more of the fat has an opportunity to leak out, so the resulting meatloaf is a bit lighter; and (3) it cooks faster. So why do we do it in a loaf pan? Tradition! Sorry, wrong Bock and Harnick musical.

 To tame the sweetness of the sweet potatoes, Georg and Amalia–style, add some acid by way of an orange. Zest the orange right into the sweet potatoes and add a squeeze of the juice, blending and tasting as you go, until it's to your liking.

LISTENING NOTES

 Did you know that the 2016 Broadway revival of *She Loves Me* starring Laura Benanti and Zachary Levi was the first Broadway show to ever be live-streamed? Trip to a movie theater to see a musical, you say? Better than "A Trip to the Library."

 There was going to be a fourth (well, at that time, third) film adaptation of *Parfumerie* in 1967 when MGM actually bought the screen rights to *She Loves Me*. It was slated to star Julie Andrews and be directed by its original director, Hal Prince. By 1969, however, MGM was being restructured and wanted to appeal to younger audiences and plans for the musical were sadly dropped. The youth, again, ruin everything.

 "Vanilla Ice Cream," one of the most beloved and famous songs from the show, wasn't added until its out-of-town tryout. Bock and Harnick auditioned the song for its original star, Barbara Cook, the very same morning she performed it at night. She reasoned that it was a letter so she wouldn't have to memorize the lyrics and, thus, was able to perform it the same day she learned it. The song was a showstopper, and a Broadway favorite was born.

The Sound of Moussaka

Eggplant and "Lonely Goatherd" Lamb Casserole

• • •

Inspired by THE SOUND OF MUSIC

Music by Richard Rodgers, *Lyrics by* Oscar Hammerstein II,
Book by Howard Lindsay *and* Russel Crouse

Opened on Broadway in 1959 at the Lunt-Fontanne Theatre

WHEN YOU KNOW THE RE . . . CI . . . PE, YOU CAN MAKE LAMB casserole. Loosely based on the 1949 memoir, *The Story of the Trapp Family Singers* by *the* Maria von Trapp, *The Sound of Music* follows a nun, Maria, who also happens to be a flibbertigibbet, a will-o'-the wisp, and a clown. Maria leaves her convent to become a governess who teaches the recalcitrant von Trapps how to sing and make clothes out of curtains. She warms the heart of the strict patriarch of the family through song and marries him, and then they all form a family band and quickly escape the Nazis together. Unbelievable? Yes, but, readers, mostly true. And here's something that's 100-percent true: Moussaka is delicious. Why are we making a Greek eggplant lasagna for a musical set in Austria? Well, the spices in a moussaka are reminiscent of spices you might find in a Viennese pastry (cinnamon, nutmeg, cloves). And dried currants, which add a tangy pop, are straight out of a Linzertorte. Don't worry, the Maria-like sweetness is tempered by the tang of the feta, a total Baroness. We promise, this'll be one of your favorite things.

FOR THE LAMB RAGU

¼ cup dried currants

¼ cup extra-virgin olive oil

2 pounds ground lamb

1 teaspoon ground cinnamon

1 teaspoon nutmeg

1 teaspoon ground allspice

½ teaspoon ground cloves

½ teaspoon cayenne pepper

1 teaspoon kosher salt

2 onions, halved and thinly sliced

5 garlic cloves, finely chopped

2 tablespoons tomato paste

1 cup red wine

One 28-ounce can plum tomatoes, puréed

1 tablespoon chopped fresh oregano

1 tablespoon chopped fresh mint

FOR THE EGGPLANT

3½ pounds eggplant, cut into ½-inch rounds

Extra-virgin olive oil

Kosher salt

Pepper

FOR THE BÉCHAMEL SAUCE

6 tablespoons unsalted butter

½ cup all-purpose flour

1 teaspoon cinnamon

1 teaspoon nutmeg

¼ teaspoon ground cloves

2½ cups whole milk

3 egg yolks

7 ounces crumbled Greek feta

1 cup grated Pecorino Romano

Lemon zest

RECIPE CONTINUES

TO MAKE THE LAMB RAGU

1. Preheat the oven to 475°F.

2. Soak the dried currants in ½ cup of warm water and set aside for 30 minutes to plump up.

3. In a large skillet or Dutch oven, heat 2 tablespoons of olive oil on high heat and, when hot, add the lamb, cinnamon, nutmeg, allspice, cloves, cayenne pepper, and salt. Cook, breaking up the meat with a wooden spoon, until nicely browned all over, about 10 minutes.

4. Scrape the lamb into a large strainer set over a bowl and drain away the fat. Discard the fat in the pan, add 3 tablespoons olive oil, then the onions plus a pinch of salt, and cook until soft. Add the garlic and tomato paste and cook, toasting the paste a bit.

5. Add the lamb back to the pan and pour in the wine, cooking until completely evaporated. Add the tomatoes and drained currants and another pinch of salt and cook until nice and thick, about 30 minutes. Stir in the oregano, mint, and salt to taste.

TO MAKE THE EGGPLANT

1. Place the eggplant rings on two baking sheets. They should be in a single layer; you may have to do this in batches. Brush the eggplant on both sides with olive oil and sprinkle all over with salt and pepper.

2. Place one of the baking sheets on the bottom of the oven and one on the middle shelf. Close the door and carefully monitor the eggplant: the hot oven floor will help develop a great color, but can easily burn. After about 5 minutes, switch the baking sheets and repeat, flipping the eggplants over when nicely browned on the bottom, until the eggplant rings are deep bronze all over and can be easily penetrated with a knife.

TO MAKE THE BÉCHAMEL SAUCE

1. Lower the oven temperature to 400°F. Start by melting the butter in a saucepan, then whisk in your flour, cinnamon, nutmeg, and cloves. Cook, on medium heat, for a minute, then slowly whisk in the milk. Keep cooking and whisking (it should be bubbling) until the béchamel begins to thicken enough to coat the back of a spoon.

2. Remove from the heat and let sit for 1 minute, then whisk in the egg yolks, the crumbled feta, ½ cup of Pecorino, and the lemon zest.

TO MAKE THE MOUSSAKA

1. Brush a 9-by-13-inch pan with olive oil. Layer in half of the roasted eggplant, top with half of the lamb ragu, cover with the remaining eggplant, and cover with the

remaining lamb ragu. Pour the béchamel over the top, smoothing with a rubber spatula, and then sprinkle over the remaining ½ cup Pecorino.

2. Bake on a baking sheet (in case any spills over) for 30 minutes, until bubbling and nicely brown on top. (If the top isn't browned to your liking, place under the broiler but keep an eye on it, until nicely bronzed.) Allow to cool for 20 minutes before cutting into squares and serving.

COOKING NOTES

 If making a moussaka sounds daunting, start at the very beginning (a very good place to start): You can make the lamb ragu and roasted eggplant and béchamel a day or two ahead and assemble everything when you're good and ready.

 How do you solve a problem like not having a wood-burning oven at home? The answer: Roasting vegetables on the bottom of the oven on a baking sheet (follow the instructions for the eggplant), which we learned from Nancy Silverton's *Mozza at Home*, a great way to get color on all kinds of roasted vegetables. Try it with cauliflower, broccoli, peppers, onions—you name it. Just coat them with olive oil, salt, and pepper first and be sure to monitor them as they cook.

LISTENING NOTES

 The Sound of Music was sadly the last musical ever written by Rodgers and Hammerstein (who together churned out some of the greatest hits of Broadway's golden age, but you already knew that). Hammerstein died of stomach cancer nine months after the musical premiered on Broadway. "Edelweiss" was the last song he ever wrote.

 Remember when we said mostly true? Well, fiction always makes a story better. One particular discrepancy from Maria's real life is that the von Trapps did not escape the Nazis by crossing the Alps. They took a train to Italy and then from there traveled to America, instead. "Climb Ev'ry Mountain"? We call B.S.!

 The design for the original Broadway show was a two-story set. Its star, Mary Martin, once wore a pedometer during a show and found out that she traversed three miles every performance. Six miles on two show days! At least we can say Mary Martin actually climbed a mountain.

Cauliflower Drum Song

A Hundred Million Granules of Cauliflower Fried "Rice"

• • •

Inspired by FLOWER DRUM SONG

Music by Richard Rodgers, *Lyrics by* Oscar Hammerstein II, *Book by* Oscar Hammerstein II, Joseph Fields, *and revised in 2002 by* David Henry Hwang

Opened on Broadway in 1958 at the St. James Theatre

WHAT ARE WE GOING TO DO ABOUT CAULIFLOWER FRIED RICE? Based on C. Y. Lee's 1957 novel, *The Flower Drum Song*, *Flower Drum Song* follows Mei Li who illegally emigrates from China to San Francisco's Chinatown. A slew of different people debate marrying her. Actually, a slew of different people debate marrying a slew of different people. It's sort of the whole plot! By the end of the show, love wins and, because we're in R and H territory, we've seen a dreamy ballet. And now for a dreamy ballet . . . in a wok: Replicating fried rice with cashews, eggs, and peas, this dish substitutes grated cauliflower for the rice itself. What you wind up with is a vegetable-forward main dish that's not in any way punishing or boring. One look at this dish and you'll be singing "You Are Beautiful" until people say, "That's weird, just eat."

2 small heads cauliflower
   (about 2 pounds)
2 tablespoons vegetable
   oil
2 large eggs, beaten
½ teaspoon kosher salt
½ cup whole cashews
1 red pepper, cut into
   small dice

1 bunch scallions, sliced,
   white and green parts
   separated
2 garlic cloves, minced
2 tablespoons peeled and
   minced fresh ginger
1 cup frozen peas (no
   need to thaw)

¼ cup low-sodium soy
   sauce
1 tablespoon fish sauce
1 tablespoon rice wine
   vinegar
1 tablespoon toasted
   sesame oil
Sriracha (optional)

1. Cut the big leaves off the cauliflower heads and any green parts. Grate the cauliflower, floret-side forward, on the largest holes of a box grater until you have 3 cups of grated cauliflower "rice." (You can use some of the core, but it won't be as flavorful.) Set aside.

2. Heat a wok or a large skillet on high heat for at least 1 minute until very hot. Swirl 1 tablespoon vegetable oil down the sides, then add the eggs and salt. Stir all around with a metal spatula and, when scrambled, remove to a plate.

3. Swirl in the remaining oil to the wok or pan. Add the cashews and sauté for 30 seconds, until just starting to brown. Add the red pepper and the white parts of the scallion and continue to cook for another 30 seconds. Add the garlic and the ginger and, just as they become fragrant, add the cauliflower and the peas.

RECIPE CONTINUES

4. Stir-fry until the cauliflower rice is starting to cook through, about 2 minutes, then add the soy sauce and fish sauce. Continue cooking until everything looks nicely combined. Off the heat, stir in the prepared eggs, rice wine vinegar, and toasted sesame oil. Garnish with sriracha (if using) and the reserved scallion greens.

COOKING NOTES

 Hate cauliflower? Too healthy? Like a god, you can change this up by using actual white rice instead of the fake stuff. Just cook white rice the day before and refrigerate overnight or use cold leftover rice from takeout. The key is that chilled rice does better here than warm rice; it helps the grains stay separate.

 We enjoy being a girl who knows how to use her leftovers. In this case, if you have leftover cauliflower fried rice, mix it with a raw egg and 2 tablespoons of flour and form into patties. You can sear them in hot oil in a skillet and serve them as a different, but still somewhat healthy, dinner.

LISTENING NOTES

 Rodgers and Hammerstein were frustrated that record producers were profiting so much from their work that they formed their own record company to produce the cast recording of *Flower Drum Song*. It sadly only sold 300,000 copies, but worry not, *The Sound of Music* was just around the corner, and let's just say it did well.

 The film adaptation of *Flower Drum Song* broke boundaries by being the first Hollywood film to have a majority Asian-American cast in a modern Asian-American story. It would be another 30 years before Hollywood attempted this again with *The Joy Luck Club* in 1993.

Rodgers and Hammerstein wanted Yul Brynner to direct the original production but he was too busy, and they ended up hiring none other than Gene Kelly.

Dreamgrills

One Bite–Only Mushroom Kabobs with You're-Gonna-Sesame Sauce

• • •

Inspired by DREAMGIRLS

Music by Henry Krieger, *Lyrics and Book by* Tom Eyen

Opened on Broadway in 1981 at the Imperial Theatre

MUSHROOM KABOBS WILL HELP YOU TO SURVIVE, MUSHROOM kabobs keep your fantasies alive! Loosely inspired by Diana Ross and the Supremes, *Dreamgirls* tells the story of Effie, Deena, and Lorrell, and charts their meteoric rise, their ups and downs, and the ousting of Effie—the pipes of the group—even though Curtis said he loved her. Success, love, family, and betrayal are electrically intertwined in this story, and the music is so toe-tapping (on the 2 and 4, people!) that audience members scream, "I'M TELLING YOU, WE'RE NOT GOING!" when the lights come up. One thing that will for sure get you going, though, are these kebabs—an exciting vegetarian entrée that takes on all the hallmarks of grilled meat without having to step to the bad side (of killing an animal). The garlic butter soy sauce adds extra umami to your mushrooms as they cook; three sources of sesame (tahini, toasted sesame oil, and sesame seeds) give an earthiness to the sauce, which also gets a boost from lime and sriracha. It'll take one bite only for you to say, "Oh my, oh my."

RECIPE CONTINUES

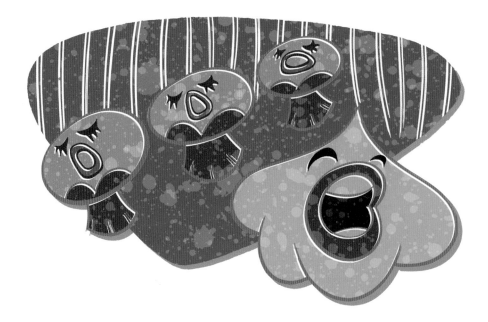

FOR THE KABOBS

4 tablespoons butter

2 garlic cloves, finely chopped

1 tablespoon soy sauce

32 baby bella, cremini, or white button mushrooms, stemmed

FOR THE SESAME SAUCE

½ cup tahini

¼ cup water

¼ cup freshly squeezed lime juice

1 teaspoon soy sauce

1 tablespoon toasted sesame oil

1 teaspoon sriracha

1 garlic clove, grated

FOR SERVING

3 cups cooked white rice

Fresh cilantro, chopped, for sprinkling

Sesame seeds

1. Soak wooden skewers in cold water for 20 minutes.

2. In a small skillet, melt the butter on high heat and add the garlic just as the butter begins to foam. Turn off the heat, add the soy sauce, and stir to distribute. Set aside.

3. Make the sesame sauce by whisking together the tahini, water, lime juice, soy sauce, toasted sesame oil, sriracha, and grated garlic. Taste to adjust for salt (more soy) and acid (more lime juice).

4. Heat a grill or a cast-iron skillet on very high heat. Skewer the mushrooms, 4 to a skewer, using two skewers to secure them. Brush them all over with the butter mixture, then lay the skewers on the very hot grill or pan. Cover for 1 minute, check

its coloring, and, when it's brown on one side, flip over and brush again with the butter mixture. Continue until the mushrooms are brown and grilled all over, 4 to 5 minutes total.

5. Fill four bowls with rice and place the skewers on top of the rice. Drizzle with the sesame sauce and sprinkle with the cilantro and sesame seeds. Serve right away.

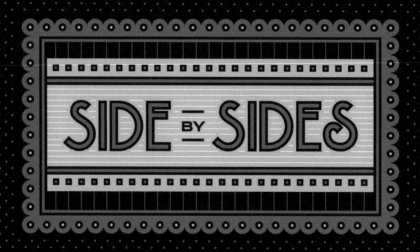

SLAWSETTOS

I'm Breaking Down a Cabbage Deli-Style Coleslaw
with Everything Bagel Seasoning

FUN(YON) HOME

Onion Ring of Keys

The LAST FIVE EARS

Summer-in-Ohio Sautéed Corn with Lime

Les BROCCOLI RABE-LES

Roasted Broccoli Rabe with
"Red and Black" Sauces

YAM YANKEES

Roasted Sweet Potato Wedges with
Whatever-Lola-Wants Sauce

Slawsettos

I'm Breaking Down a Cabbage Deli-Style Coleslaw with Everything Bagel Seasoning

• • •

Inspired by FALSETTOS

Music and Lyrics by William Finn, *Book by* William Finn *and* James Lapine

Opened on Broadway in 1992 at the John Golden Theatre

CAN YOU TELL WE HAVE BEEN REVISED? THIS 'SLAW'S SO SWELL, but we are not surprised. *Falsettos* consists of two one-act musicals—Finn's 1981 *March of the Falsettos* and Finn and Lapine's 1990 *Falsettoland*. This sweet and melancholic musical follows Marvin who, after leaving his wife and son for a man named Whizzer, tries to navigate an unconventional family life amid the AIDS epidemic. Marvin's ex-wife, Trina, ends up marrying Marvin's psychiatrist, his son gets bar mitzvahed and plays baseball, there are two lesbians next door, and sadly, we ultimately lose Whizzer, which is a painful reminder that today could always be your last day to eat coleslaw, so get to it. The secret to this coleslaw is shredding the cabbage as thinly as possible: A mandoline is the best tool for that, the shredding disc on a food processor the second-best tool. The goal here is to create a deli-style coleslaw that Marvin might pick up on his way home from the psychiatrist. And, in honor of "Four Jews in a Room Bitching," we've added the four everything bagel spices: poppy seeds, sesame seeds, dried minced onion, and dried minced garlic. The resulting coleslaw is truly a miracle of Judaism.

1 medium green cabbage (about the size of a bowling ball), sliced in half, cored

4 carrots, peeled, tops removed

½ cup mayonnaise

1 tablespoon Dijon mustard

½ cup cider vinegar

1 teaspoon celery salt

½ teaspoon freshly ground black pepper

½ cup chopped Italian flat-leaf parsley

½ cup chopped fresh dill

1 tablespoon poppy seeds*

1 tablespoon sesame seeds

1 tablespoon dried minced garlic

1 tablespoon dried minced onion

Kosher salt (optional)

*Tip: To avoid having to buy poppy seeds, sesame seeds, dried minced garlic, and dried minced onion, consider buying Trader Joe's Everything Bagel Seasoning and use 4 tablespoons of that.

1. Either by hand, with a mandoline, or using the shredding disc of your food processor (a much easier method!), finely shred the cabbage and place in a large bowl. Switch to the grating disc (or use a hand grater) and grate the carrots, adding to the cabbage.

2. Using tongs (or your hands), mix in the mayonnaise, mustard, cider vinegar, celery salt, pepper, parsley, and dill.

3. In a small bowl, combine the poppy seeds, sesame seeds, dried minced garlic, and dried minced onion. Pour half of the mixture into the coleslaw and mix it through, tasting as you go, and adjusting with more salt and vinegar if necessary.

4. Sprinkle with the reserved everything bagel seasoning and serve.

RECIPE CONTINUES

If your kosher catering business needs a little more flair, try using a mixture of green and purple cabbage. You can also add sliced multicolored radishes, use multicolored carrots, and, if you want onion breath (and what Jewish person doesn't?), add sliced red onion or scallions.

 For a lighter version, you can skip the mayo and add ¼ cup of olive oil instead. But you gotta die sometime, so why skip it?

LISTENING NOTES

 There is a third one-act musical that is not included in *Falsettos* called *In Trousers,* which takes place before Marvin meets Whizzer and deals with Marvin coming to terms with his sexuality. We guess *Star Wars* isn't the only entertainment here with prequels . . .

 The haftorah that Jason reads at his bar mitzvah was originally the same haftorah that Finn read at his own bar mitzvah, until Finn took some liberties and zhuzhed it up.

 The original producers of *Falsettos* were worried that the subject matter wouldn't be commercial enough to bring in audiences. They wanted to emulate the success of *Les Misérables* and *Miss Saigon*'s instantly recognizable logos, and settled on a Keith Haring design in which two adults and a child are holding up a heart.

Fun(yon) Home

Onion Ring of Keys

• • •

Inspired by FUN HOME

Music by Jeanine Tesori, *Lyrics and Book by* Lisa Kron

Opened on Broadway in 2015 at the Circle in the Square Theatre

'M CHANGING MY MAJOR TO COOKING ONION RINGS, WITH A MINOR in eating onion rings, foreign study to digesting onion rings. Based on Alison Bechdel's graphic novel of the same name (and yes, it does pass the Bechdel test—*phew*), *Fun Home* is a retrospective of Bechdel's life and her relationship with her father, a closeted gay man, all told through small, medium, and regular versions of herself (like Goldilocks and the three bears . . . but for lesbians). But seriously, *Fun Home* is an incredibly moving musical that broke boundaries in 2015 by being the first Broadway musical to ever feature a lesbian protagonist, because lord knows Broadway has had enough gay male protagonists! And lesbian protagonists love nothing more than onion rings (rough transition, we know). These are a cinch to make—with a beer-based batter (because the characters in *Fun Home* drink beer) and lots of spices—the only stressful part is lowering them into the hot oil. As long as you're confident and lay the onion rings away from you as they hit the oil, all will go fine, and you'll have truly excellent onion rings to share with all three versions of yourself.

RECIPE CONTINUES

2½ cups all-purpose flour
½ cup cornstarch
2 teaspoons garlic powder
2 teaspoons chili powder
1 teaspoon cayenne pepper

½ teaspoon freshly ground black pepper
1 tablespoon kosher salt, plus more for sprinkling
2½ cups beer
1 egg

Dash of Worcestershire sauce
1 quart canola oil
3 large yellow onions, peeled, sliced into ½-inch rings

1. Heat the oven to 250°F.

2. Whisk together the flour, cornstarch, garlic powder, chili powder, cayenne, black pepper, and salt. Slowly whisk in the beer, then the egg, and finally the Worcestershire until it forms a smooth, thick batter.

3. Set cooling racks over two foil-lined rimmed sheet pans (makes them easier to clean). In a deep pot or Dutch oven (the oil should come up at least an inch), heat the canola oil until it reaches 350°F on a deep-fry thermometer.

4. Working in batches, dip your rings into the batter, let excess drip off, and carefully lower into the oil. (It works best to add them one at a time; five or six per batch, making sure to maintain the oil temperature.) Cook them for 2 to 3 minutes, until golden brown all over, then remove with tongs to the cooling racks and sprinkle with a little extra salt. Keep warm in the oven until all your onion rings are fried.

Not too bad, if we say so ourselves, to eat these onion rings all alone. But they're even better with a dipping sauce. Try combining 1 cup mayonnaise, 1 tablespoon horseradish, ¼ cup ketchup, 1 tablespoon sriracha, a pinch of salt and pepper, and a squeeze of lemon juice for something bright and zippy.

 Should you have extra batter, put on your party dress (or overalls, you decide) and drop in some thickly sliced zucchini, cauliflower florets, or anything else that's not too watery (water and hot oil don't mix) into the batter, then lower into the oil and fry until golden brown and cooked through.

 Because of scheduling conflicts, Bechdel ended up missing the Off-Broadway premiere of *Fun Home* and consequently made a comic strip about the experience. Could this be material for a sequel to *Fun Home*? Probably not.

 Fun Home, the graphic novel, was lauded by critics. However, due to its honest depiction of gay life, the novel was banned for a time from one of Missouri's public libraries, boycotted by freshmen at Duke University, and almost banned from the University of Utah and the College of Charleston's syllabus. Ah, progress . . .

 Did you know that Lisa Kron and Jeanine Tesori are the first female writing team to ever win the Tony Award for Best Original Score of a Musical? Cyndi Lauper was the first solo female win in 2013 for *Kinky Boots.*

The Last Five Ears

Summer in Ohio Sautéed Corn with Lime

• • •

Inspired by THE LAST FIVE YEARS

Music, Book, and Lyrics by Jason Robert Brown

Opened Off-Broadway in 2002 at the Minette Theatre

W ON'T YOU MAKE SOME CORN WITH US, FOR THE NEXT TEN minutes? *The Last Five Years* is an original musical about a man and woman sitting on stools who happen to break through the time space continuum. We see their relationship unfold and crumble as the man, Jamie, moves forward in time, and the woman, Cathy, moves backward in time. And look, it doesn't end well, but most relationships don't, especially when they involve narcissistic writers who have little patience for actresses. Haunting, funny, and sad, *The Last Five Years* has provided musical theater performers top-notch up-tempos and ballads since its Off-Broadway inception in 2002. It also provided the inspiration for this dish, which involves fresh summer corn, a stripper, Wayne the snake, and Mrs. Jamie Wellerstein, that's me! Sorry, we got sidetracked. Sauté the fresh corn kernels in lots of butter with a shallot, habanero, and cilantro stems, add some lime juice and Aleppo pepper at the end, and a miracle will happen in your mouth.

3 tablespoons butter

5 ears of corn, husked, cut off the cob (about 5 cups)

1 tablespoon kosher salt

1 shallot, minced

1 habanero, seeded, minced (optional)

1 bunch cilantro, stems sliced thinly, leaves reserved

1 teaspoon freshly ground black pepper

Juice of 2 limes

Aleppo pepper (optional)

1. In a large skillet, melt the butter on high heat. When the foam subsides, add all the corn, sprinkle with the salt, and stir and cook on high heat until the corn is cooked through and starting to brown a bit, 4 to 5 minutes. Add the shallot, habanero (if using), and the cilantro stems, stir all around, and cook for another minute.

2. Off the heat, add the black pepper and lime juice. Stir in half of the cilantro leaves, then sprinkle with Aleppo pepper (which adds a fruity heat and some color). Taste and adjust for salt and acid (lime juice). Sprinkle the remaining cilantro leaves on top and serve right away.

RECIPE CONTINUES

Still hurting from corn kernels flying everywhere? Here's a great trick for cutting fresh corn off the cob. Take a large mixing bowl and place a smaller bowl (like a cereal bowl) inside it upside-down. Place the corn on top of the smaller bowl and cut, with a very sharp knife, straight down. The kernels will hit the side of the larger bowl and not go flying all around your kitchen.

 This dish is definitely best made at the height of summer with sweet, freshly shucked summer corn. But when it's time to say goodbye until tomorrow . . . to summer, you *can* make this recipe with frozen corn. You'll want to take the first step a bit further, though, and try to get it brown when sautéing it to help sweeten it up.

 This is the only musical included in this book that has never made it to Broadway (at *Swiss Chards'* publication, that is). We're sorry if this upsets any of our readers, but what can we say? Like Cathy, we're a glutton for punishment.

 Jason Robert Brown was sued by his ex-wife for representing their relationship too closely, so to settle the matter, he rewrote a song about his ex-wife called "I Could Be in Love with Someone Like You" and turned it into "Shiksa Goddess." So, if you love that song, you have Jason's divorce lawyer to thank.

 Cathy and Jamie don't interact at all throughout the musical, except halfway through when their storylines intersect in "The Next Ten Minutes." In a beautiful and ingenious song, Jamie proposes and then they proceed to get married and share their vows.

Les Broccoli Rabe-les

Roasted Broccoli Rabe with "Red and Black" Sauces

• • •

Inspired by LES MISÉRABLES

Music by Claude-Michel Schönberg, *Original French Lyrics by* Alain Boublil *and* Jean-Marc Natel, *Original English Lyrics by* Herbert Kretzmer, *Book by* Claude-Michel Schönberg *and* Alain Boublil

Opened on Broadway in 1987 at the Broadway Theatre

LOOK DOWN! LOOK DOWN! THERE'S BROCCOLI RABE IN YOUR dish. This mega musical, based on Victor Hugo's 1862 novel *Les Misérables*, follows French peasant Jean Valjean, who breaks parole after serving 19 years in prison for stealing a loaf of bread (sure hope that was a good loaf of bread). Valjean encounters a dying prostitute named Fantine and raises her daughter, Cosette. Cosette later enters a love triangle with a strapping young man, Marius and tragic heroine with a dynamite solo, Éponine, and then stumbles into a barricade of revolutionaries, all while constantly being trailed by overly obsessive police inspector Javert (chill, Javert). If that plot seems tangly and complex, it still yielded one of the most successful musicals of all time. And speaking of things that are tangly and complex, time to welcome broccoli rabe into your kitchen. This tangly, green vegetable is way more interesting than boring old broccoli (more Éponine, less Cosette . . . sorry Cosette) and here, we coax out lots of flavor through roasting and then with a drizzle of two sauces (red, like the blood of angry men and black, like the dark of ages past). Serve this at dinner and you'll be the master of your house in no time.

RECIPE CONTINUES

2 bunches broccoli rabe, bottom stems removed, then chopped into 1-inch pieces

¼ cup extra-virgin olive oil

1 teaspoon salt

5 single-head black garlic cloves, peeled

1 tablespoon brown sugar

3 tablespoons vegetable oil

1 tablespoon soy sauce

1 teaspoon toasted sesame oil

1 tablespoon water

¼ cup rice wine or sherry vinegar

Sriracha

Sesame seeds, for sprinkling

1. Preheat the oven to 425°F.

2. In a large bowl, toss the broccoli rabe with the olive oil and salt. Lay them out on two baking sheets, making sure the broccoli rabe is spaced apart and not at all crowded.

3. Roast the broccoli rabe for 10 to 15 minutes, tossing halfway through, until golden brown all over and cooked through. (Note: It will shrink a lot. That's okay!)

4. While it cools, make the black garlic sauce by blending the black garlic, brown sugar, vegetable oil, soy sauce, toasted sesame oil, water, and vinegar in the blender.

5. To serve, place the roasted broccoli rabe on a platter and drizzle the black garlic sauce all over it, then drizzle several squiggles of sriracha. Finish with sesame seeds and serve right away.

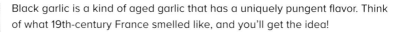
 Black garlic is a kind of aged garlic that has a uniquely pungent flavor. Think of what 19th-century France smelled like, and you'll get the idea!

 If you don't like broccoli rabe, you can make this recipe with boring old broccoli . . . don't worry, it'll still be good. There won't be empty chairs at empty tables.

LISTENING NOTES

 Did you know that, despite early mixed reviews, *Les Misérables,* at the time of *Swiss Chards*' publication, is currently the longest running show of all time on the West End?

 In the French language concept album of the musical, Fantine sang two songs that were very similar, the legendary "I Dreamed a Dream," and another song called "The Poverty Song." For the English version, Cameron Mackintosh decided to repurpose "The Poverty Song" into another legendary ditty, "On My Own." Misery really churns out great power ballads. Both are worth a listen, but proceed with caution—they're addictive.

 Les Misérables' reach goes beyond just super fans! "Do You Hear the People Sing?" has been used as a protest song by citizens of China, Turkey, Taiwan, South Korea, Belarus, the Philippines, Australia, and . . . Wisconsin.

Yam Yankees

Roasted Sweet Potato Wedges with Whatever-Lola-Wants Sauce

• • •

Inspired by DAMN YANKEES

Music by Richard Adler, *Lyrics by* Jerry Ross,
Book by George Abbott *and* Douglass Wallop

Opened on Broadway in 1955 at the 46th Street Theatre

YOU'VE GOTTA HAVE SWEET POTATO WEDGES, ALL YOU REALLY need is sweet potato wedges! Based on Wallop's 1954 novel, *The Year the Yankees Lost the Pennant*, *Damn Yankees* follows Joe Boyd who, in a Faustian bargain, sells his soul to the devil (with a negotiated exit clause—love a good deal) to become a newbie slugger for the DC Senators in order to beat those damn Yankees! Joe is transformed into a young hunk (*thank God!*), brings the team from zero to hero, thwarts off succubus with a heart of gold Lola, and just in the nick of time, transforms back to his middle-aged self. He still manages to help win the pennant for the Senators, though, even in that middle-aged body! You won't have to make a deal with the devil to eat these sweet potatoes, however. Wholesome sweet potato wedges get roasted with lots of spices in a devilishly hot oven. Then they're shamelessly drizzled with our spicy, sexy Lola sauce, but have no fear: These sweet potatoes won't give in. If the heat is too much for you, leave out the jalapeño, or just make this six months out of every year.

FOR THE SWEET POTATOES

3 medium sweet potatoes, approximately 2½ pounds

¼ cup olive oil

1 tablespoon kosher salt

1 tablespoon coriander seeds, crushed in a mortar and pestle

1 tablespoon cumin seeds, crushed in a mortar and pestle

½ teaspoon cinnamon

½ teaspoon cayenne pepper (1 teaspoon if you're feeling extra devious)

½ teaspoon freshly cracked black pepper

FOR THE LOLA SAUCE

Leaves from two bunches of cilantro, roughly chopped (about 2 cups) (it's okay if some of the stem gets in there)

1 jalapeño, halved, membranes and seeds removed, roughly chopped

4 garlic cloves, peeled and roughly chopped

1 teaspoon kosher salt

½ cup freshly squeezed lime juice

¼ cup olive oil

RECIPE CONTINUES

1. Preheat the oven to 425°F.

2. Wash and dry the sweet potatoes well. Leaving the skin on and using a large sharp knife, slice the sweet potatoes in half lengthwise. Cut each half in half again and then one more time. You should have eight wedges per sweet potato.

3. In a large bowl, toss the sweet potato wedges with the olive oil, salt, crushed coriander seeds, crushed cumin seeds, cinnamon, cayenne pepper, and black pepper so that everything is coated well.

4. Place the sweet potatoes, flesh-side down, on a large baking sheet and roast in the oven for 30 to 40 minutes, turning them every 10 minutes or so in order to get all the sides golden brown. Keep an eye on them—the sugar in the sweet potatoes has a tendency to burn. When the potatoes are crisp all over and a knife goes through easily, remove them from the oven.

TO MAKE THE LOLA SAUCE

1. Make the Lola sauce by blitzing the cilantro leaves, jalapeño, garlic, and salt in the bowl of a food processor (5 to 6 blitzes). Pour in the lime juice and olive oil and blitz until it makes a rough-looking sauce. Taste and adjust with more salt and/or lime juice.

TO SERVE

1. Place the sweet potato wedges on a platter and dollop the Lola sauce on top, conserving some to serve alongside in a small bowl. Eat right away.

This technique would also work well with winter squash: Try it with a delicata sliced into rings. (World Series rings, if possible.) The cooking time may vary, so keep an eye on them.

 If you want to transform this into more traditional breakfast home fries, cut the sweet potatoes into cubes, toss with the same mixture of olive oil and spices, and roast on a baking sheet at 425°F, tossing every few minutes until crisp all over, 20 to 30 minutes. Top with fried eggs and a bit of the Lola sauce. Now who's got the brains and the talent?

LISTENING NOTES

 This was the first show that Gwen Verdon and Bob Fosse worked on together. It was the start of a long, vital, and tumultuous artistic and personal relationship. You can see them dancing together in a genius performance of "Who's Got the Pain?" (fitting title . . .) in the film adaptation. You can learn more about their relationship on the FX show, *Fosse/Verdon*.

 In the film, every principal role but Joe Hardy was cast directly from the Broadway musical. Movie producers . . . take note!

 The original cast album for *Damn Yankees* featured Gwen Verdon in a baseball shirt in front of a green background; however, shrewd producers quickly decided to take that off the market and to replace the cover with Gwen in a provocative Lola costume in front of a red background instead. And guess what? They started selling like hotcakes.

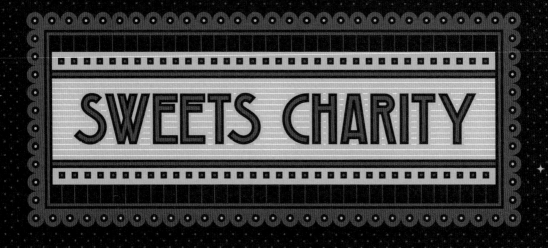

Wickedoodles

Snickerdoodles with Elphaba Green Matcha

• • •

Inspired by WICKED

Music and Lyrics by Stephen Schwartz, *Book by* Winnie Holzman

Opened on Broadway in 2003 at the Gershwin Theatre

DID THAT REALLY JUST HAPPEN? HAVE WE ACTUALLY MADE THE world's best snickerdoodles? Based on Gregory Maguire's 1995 novel, *Wicked: The Life and Times of the Wicked Witch of the West*, *Wicked* tells the story of Elphaba, the misunderstood villainess of *The Wizard of Oz*. In *Wicked*, Elphaba ain't evil, she's just a green-skinned outcast who deeply cares about animal rights. She uncovers a mass conspiracy to suppress "animal speak" headed by her headmistress and the Wizard of Oz himself, and they decide to deflect the blame and scapegoat Elphaba for their misdeeds. Fascist government scapegoating powerful women? Tale as old as time. Take heart, though—these Wickedoodles will empower you to defy gravity and topple fascist governments, money back guaranteed. Like the traditional snickerdoodle, these are made with butter, sugar, eggs, and cream of tartar. If you're wondering *what is this feeling?* when you eat them, that's matcha, which is green tea powder. It's used instead of cinnamon. It adds depth-of-flavor and a faint green color, which we enhance with green food coloring (no de-greenifying here!). Once everyone gets a taste, they'll be grabbing them off the tray like witch hunters. Thank goodness this makes 12.

Bernadette Peters replaced Catherine Zeta-Jones in the 2009 Broadway revival, and whole almonds could easily replace the pistachios here. Just roughly chop them the same way and proceed with the recipe.

 Perpetual anticipation may make it hard not to eat all the pistachio brittle right away when you make it, but if you save some, you can break it up and sprinkle it over vanilla ice cream.

LISTENING NOTES

 "Send In the Clowns," the show's most famous song, was written more as an afterthought. Sondheim wrote it days before *A Little Night Music*'s out-of-town tryout when he discovered that Glynis Johns, the original Desiree, could *sort of* sing. Despite not being able to properly sustain a phrase, Sondheim used Johns' "weaknesses" and devised this song to end in consonants, which would give the lines in the song short cutoffs and thus be easier to sustain. The song is entirely written in short phrases meant more to be acted than sung. Tell that to Barbra Streisand . . .

 To be evocative of Sweden in the 1900s, Sondheim wrote most of *A Little Night Music*'s music in Waltz meter (three-quarter time). Because that's what geniuses do.

 The film adaptation of *A Little Night Music* starred Elizabeth Taylor and was reset in Austria and not Sweden. The movie was a big flop, which teaches us the lesson to never turn your back on Sweden.

1 cup granulated sugar
½ cup light corn syrup
¼ cup water
½ teaspoon kosher salt

2 tablespoons unsalted butter
½ teaspoon baking soda

1½ cups roasted, shelled, salted pistachios, roughly chopped
1 tablespoon Maldon sea salt

1. Line a 9-by-13-inch baking sheet with parchment paper and spray with a light coating of nonstick cooking spray.

2. In a medium pot, combine the sugar, corn syrup, water, and salt. Whisk and then bring the mixture to a boil over high heat—being extra careful because sticky, boiling hot sugar will burn you bad. Cook, without stirring, until the mixture turns golden and reaches 300°F on a candy thermometer.

3. Remove from the heat and very carefully add the butter, baking soda, and pistachios. Stir everything with a heatproof rubber spatula, then pour on the prepared baking sheet. Working very quickly, spread thin with an offset spatula sprayed with cooking spray and then sprinkle with the Maldon sea salt. Allow to cool completely (about 20 minutes), then break into pieces. The brittle will keep for several days in an airtight container.

A Brittle Bite Music

Isn't-It-Rich? Salted Pistachio Brittle

• • •

Inspired by A LITTLE NIGHT MUSIC

Music and Lyrics by Stephen Sondheim, *Book by* Hugh Wheeler

Opened on Broadway in 1973 at the Shubert Theatre

EVERY DAY A LITTLE BRITTLE, IN THE PARLOR, IN THE BED. Based on the 1955 Ingmar Bergman film, *Smiles of a Summer Night*, *A Little Night Music* follows rich Swedish folk in the country who all sleep with each other. Oh, to be rich and Swedish. There's an actress Desiree, who's obsessed with clowns and still deeply pines for old flame Fredrik, whose son Henrik runs away with his own stepmother Anne, all while Desiree's grande dame mother Madam Armfeldt sits in a wheelchair and watches as love's wrongs are righted and then dies. She might have eaten this brittle, because reader, it's to die for! With bright green pistachios, butter, and Maldon sea salt for an extra thrill, this brittle is the perfect treat to bring for a weekend in the country. You can eat them now, later, or soon, but just be careful when making them, because not only is the caramel hot, it'll stick to you and burn you at the same time . . . sort of like some of the characters in this show. The results are worth the effort, but don't eat too much: It's a very short road from the pinch and the punch to the paunch and the pouch and the pension.

RECIPE CONTINUES

If you want your champagne Jell-O to put on its Sunday clothes, you could add pomegranate seeds in addition to the raspberries for more pizzazz. Other options include blueberries, melon balls, and blackberries. Also try adding a ¼ cup of Chambord or Framboise in place of the same amount of the Prosecco to emphasize the raspberry flavor. It will tinge your Jell-O red.

 It only takes a moment for the Jell-O to go wrong. If yours doesn't set, you probably need to heat it up again and add another packet of gelatin. Simply pour it back into the mold when done, and you'll be galloping with your tray of Jell-O in no time.

LISTENING NOTES

 The original production once held the title of the longest running musical and third longest running show in Broadway history. Need a hit? Call on Dolly . . .

 In 1967, the *Hello, Dolly!* cast was entirely replaced by an all-Black cast led by the incomparable Pearl Bailey. Pearl also led a revival of the musical with an all-Black cast in 1975.

 In 1964, the titular song, "Hello, Dolly!" was covered by Louis Armstrong, and rose to the top spot in the Billboard Pop chart, making him the oldest person to ever accomplish such a thing at 62. 62? Dolly would be proud.

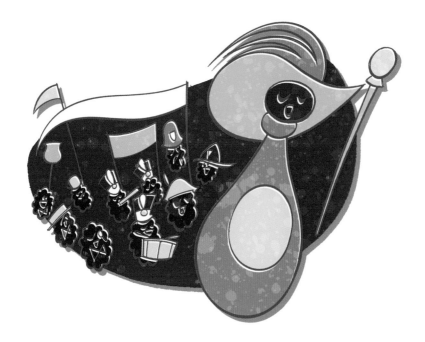

One 750 milliliter bottle chilled sparkling wine (Prosecco works great)

3 envelopes unflavored powdered gelatin

⅔ cup granulated sugar

¼ cup fresh lemon juice

1 cup fresh raspberries

1. Lightly spray a 6-cup mold or Bundt pan with nonstick spray and set aside.

2. In a 3- to 4-quart saucepan, pour in the sparkling wine and stir in the gelatin, sugar, and lemon juice. Allow to sit for 5 minutes, then heat on medium heat, whisking, until the sugar and gelatin are dissolved and the liquid just starts to bubble on the side. Set aside for 5 minutes, then pour into the mold.

3. Refrigerate the mold until the Jell-O starts to thicken, anywhere from 20 to 40 minutes. Press in the raspberries throughout the mold in various places, keeping in mind that the finished dish will be upside-down.

4. Cover with plastic wrap and refrigerate overnight (or at least 6 hours). When ready to unmold, fill a large bowl with warm water and dip the mold into the water for a few seconds. Tilt the pan to see if the Jell-O is starting to release. Flip out onto a cake stand and serve right away.

RECIPE CONTINUES

Jell-O, Dolly!

Before-the-Gelée-Passes-By Champagne Jell-O with Raspberries

• • •

Inspired by HELLO, DOLLY!

Music and Lyrics by Jerry Herman, *Book by* Michael Stewart

Opened on Broadway in 1964 at the St. James Theatre

IT TAKES A JELL-O, A CHAMPAGNE JELL-O, TO BRING YOU THE SWEET things in life! Based on Thornton Wilder's 1938 farce, *The Merchant of Yonkers*, later revised and retitled to *The Matchmaker* in 1955, *Hello, Dolly!* follows said matchmaker, middle-aged Dolly Levi, who travels from Yonkers to NYC to find a match for grumpy "half-a-millionaire" Horace Vandergelder, which is all really a ruse to procure Horace for herself. We love an enterprising woman. No, we really do. We also love this dessert, a throwback to the Jell-O molds of yore. Warning: This isn't for your kids. This one is made with sparkling wine, with pops of fresh raspberries, a nice decorative touch, like ribbons down my back. Your back. Its back. Whatever! Serve by itself or with more fruit sprinkled on top. Whether it's for a dinner party, a parade, or a wedding, this dessert's got elegance.

2½ cups all-purpose flour

2 teaspoons cream of tartar

½ teaspoon baking soda

½ teaspoon kosher salt

3 tablespoons matcha powder

2 sticks (1 cup) butter, room temperature

1 cup granulated sugar plus ½ cup for later

½ cup packed light brown sugar

2 extra-large eggs, room temperature

1 teaspoon pure vanilla extract

1 teaspoon green food coloring

1. Preheat the oven to 350°F and line a baking sheet with parchment paper.

2. In a bowl, sift together the flour, cream of tartar, baking soda, salt, and matcha powder.

3. In the bowl of a stand mixer, beat the butter, 1 cup granulated sugar, and brown sugar. When light and fluffy (2 to 3 minutes), add the eggs one at a time, then the vanilla and green food coloring, beating until completely incorporated. Slowly add the flour mixture and beat until just combined.

RECIPE CONTINUES

4. Pour the ½ cup sugar into a bowl. Using a small ice cream scoop (¼ cup), scoop the cookies into balls and roll in the sugar, then place on the prepared baking sheets, flattening slightly with your hand.

5. Bake for 10 to 12 minutes, until the cookies are light golden. Allow to cool for 10 minutes.

 Parents: Take note that 3 tablespoons of matcha contains a good hit of caffeine! If you don't want your kids dancing through life right before bed, consider serving these cookies in the morning or, if you're concerned, seek out decaffeinated matcha powder.

 If you'd like to stick to all-natural ingredients and food coloring wigs you out, just skip it. The matcha powder will make flecks of green that'll get the job done, but the cookies won't be as pop-u-lar.

LISTENING NOTES

 Listen to the first couple of notes of the "Unlimited/ I'm Limited" portion of "Defying Gravity." The first seven notes are actually the first seven notes of "Somewhere Over the Rainbow." If Schwartz had gone any further and used the eighth note, it would have been copyright infringement. One note away from danger. Sort of like the last screlt in "Defying Gravity."

 Although Elphaba was nameless in L. Frank Baum's *Wizard of Oz*, Maguire decided to honor the original author in his book by using his initials, L.F.B., to inspire the girl with the verdigris's name.

 Wicked was the first show on the West End to ever gross more than £1 million. They were really seeing green.

Clafoutis and the Beast

Tale-as-Old-as-Thyme Pear Custard Tart with Rosewater

• • •

Inspired by BEAUTY AND THE BEAST

Music by Alan Menke*n*, *Lyrics by* Howard Ashman *and* Tim Rice*,*
Book by Linda Woolverton

Opened on Broadway in 1994 at the Palace Theatre

E'LL BE COOKING AGAIN, BE GOOD-LOOKING AGAIN, WITH a pear tart on each arm! Based on the Disney film of the same name, which in turn was based on the classic French fairy tale of the same name, *Beauty and the Beast* tells the tale of Belle, the beauty (duh), who's imprisoned by the Beast, a young selfish prince who was cursed to live his existence as a monstrous animal (hot). Love vanquishes the curse, the beast turns back into a hunk, the flamboyant candelabra turns back into a maître d', and they all live happily ever after. Especially when they find this clafoutis on the table (don't worry, it's not actually alive). It may seem intimidating, but fear not: A clafoutis is like a cross between a pudding and a pancake. Strange, no question, but trust us, it's a cinch to make. Riffing on Julia Child's classic recipe, this clafoutis has autumnal pears, woodsy thyme, and just a whisper of rose, which casts a spell over the whole thing. It may not look like much when it comes out of the oven, but sprinkled with confectioners' sugar and served slightly warm, we promise . . . there's something there.

RECIPE CONTINUES

1 tablespoon unsalted
  butter, at room
  temperature
1¼ cups whole milk
3 large eggs
⅓ cup granulated sugar
  plus 1 tablespoon

1 tablespoon vanilla
  extract
½ teaspoon rosewater
½ teaspoon kosher salt
1 tablespoon chopped
  fresh thyme

Lemon zest from 1 lemon
½ cup all-purpose flour
3 ripe but firm Comice or
  Bartlett pears, cored,
  peeled, and thinly
  sliced
Confectioners' sugar

1. Preheat the oven to 375°F.

2. Rub a 9-inch cast-iron skillet or springform pan all over with the unsalted butter and set aside.

3. In a large bowl, whisk together the milk, eggs, sugar, vanilla extract, rosewater, salt, thyme, lemon zest, and flour by hand for 1 full minute until foamy. (If you're not scared of raw egg, you can taste here to see if the rosewater is coming through. You definitely don't want to add too much—it can be overpowering—so try adding another ¼ teaspoon at a time until you just get a sense of it.)

4. Pour ¼ inch of the batter into the skillet, put on low heat, and cook just until a film forms. Remove from the heat. (If using a springform pan, pour in ¼ inch of batter and place in the oven until just set.)

5. Layer in the pears—you can make a pattern if you'd like, but it's not necessary—and sprinkle with the remaining tablespoon of sugar. Pour the rest of the batter on top and bake for 50 minutes or until the top is puffed, the edges are starting to brown, and a tester comes out clean.

6. Dust with confectioners' sugar right before serving.

=== COOKING NOTES ===

 To really make this dessert the belle of the ball, broil it at the very end just until it's a deep bronze color on top. Keep an eye on it, though, or it'll be a beast to clean up.

 To make this dessert more adult, skip the rosewater and add a tablespoon of booze: cognac, brandy, and rum all work great. Just be sure to put Chip to bed before serving.

LISTENING NOTES

 In 1998, "A Change in Me" was added to the show specifically for Toni Braxton who joined the cast as Belle, four years after the show officially opened. The song has stayed in ever since.

 The Broadway musical is considered a hybrid between the 1991 Disney cartoon by Howard Ashman and Alan Menken and new work by Alan Menken and Tim Rice. Howard Ashman sadly succumbed to AIDS before the film adaptation officially opened, and Tim Rice came on to the project to pad out the score for its 1994 Broadway premiere.

 In 2002, a very special chipped teacup was played by a very special boy named Nick Jonas.

A Chorus Lime Pie

At-the-Sorbet Frozen Key Lime Pie

• • •

Inspired by **A CHORUS LINE**

Music by Marvin Hamlisch, *Lyrics by* Edward Kleban, *Book by* James Kirkwood, Jr. *and* Nicholas Dante

Opened on Broadway in 1975 at the Shubert Theatre

ONE SINGULAR LIME PIE, EVERY LITTLE SLICE YOU EAT. BASED on hours upon hours of recorded interviews with real Broadway dancers, *A Chorus Line* electrified Broadway with its innovative storytelling by exploring the inner lives of 17 Broadway dancers vying to be in a chorus line. All provoked by Zach, the director, the dancers each share deeply personal aspects of their lives and careers—a drag performance, plastic surgery, and a crappy acting teacher, to name a few. There's also a veteran dancer from Zach's past who just wants to dance, because goodness she's a dancer, and a dancer dances! And the exciting part about this dish is that all your guests will be forming a long line (hopefully in gold lamé) waiting to receive a plate. It eats 10 and looks 10, too. So what is it? Picture it, you're on a bobsled, and instead of baking a normal key lime pie, you're baking the graham cracker crust, but then churning the filling in an ice cream maker. It's a quick number with condensed milk, whipping cream, and lime juice that yields something like an ice cream cake but in pie form. It's so easy to make, anyone who watches you will surely be thinking, "I can do that."

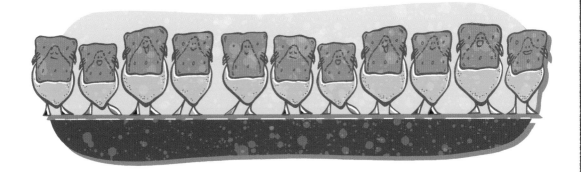

FOR THE CRUST

10 to 12 graham crackers (we like Nabisco)

2 tablespoons granulated sugar

1 teaspoon kosher salt

6 tablespoons butter, melted

FOR THE "SORBET"

One 14-ounce can sweetened condensed milk

1½ cups heavy whipping cream

1 cup freshly squeezed lime juice

1 tablespoon lime zest

½ teaspoon kosher salt

TO SERVE

1 cup heavy whipping cream

1 tablespoon granulated sugar

1 teaspoon pure vanilla extract

Lime zest, for garnish

TO MAKE THE CRUST

1. Preheat the oven to 350°F.

2. Pulse the graham crackers in a food processor until you have 1½ cups of graham cracker crumbs (the mixture should look like sand).

3. With a rubber spatula, mix together the graham cracker crumbs, sugar, salt, and melted butter.

4. Using a large measuring cup, press the mixture into a 9-inch pie plate, creating an even border along the sides. Bake for 10 minutes, until it starts to brown. Cool completely, then place in the freezer.

TO MAKE THE "SORBET"

1. In a large bowl or measuring glass, whisk together the sweetened condensed milk, heavy cream, lime juice, lime zest, and salt.

RECIPE CONTINUES

2. Pour into your ice cream maker and churn according to the manufacturer's instructions, 15 to 20 minutes, until the mixture is thick and looks like softened ice cream.

3. Immediately scrape into the now-cool graham cracker crust, smoothing it at the top with a rubber spatula. Cover loosely with plastic and place in the freezer for several hours, preferably overnight.

TO SERVE

1. Pour the heavy whipping cream, sugar, and vanilla extract in the bowl of a stand mixer with the whisk attachment and whisk on medium-high speed until soft peaks form. (You could also do this by hand in a very cold bowl.)

2. Dollop the whipped cream into the center of the pie, leaving some of the lime ice cream exposed, and zest a lime directly over the pie to garnish. Serve right away.

COOKING NOTES

 If you really couldn't churn, could never really churn, don't worry—you don't need an ice cream maker to make this. Just buy a lime ice cream or gelato (Talenti and Ciao Bella make them), soften for a bit until it's spreadable, then spread in your cooled graham cracker crust. Allow to set up in the freezer, then top with the whipped cream and lime zest.

 Bored with lime? This technique would work equally well with any fruity ice cream flavor. Audition strawberry or orange sherbet until you find one singular sensation.

LISTENING NOTES

 Eight of the Broadway dancers who were interviewed by *A Chorus Line*'s creator, Michael Bennett, were actual performers in the original production. Curious how the other dancers not asked to be in the show felt about that . . .

 By the end of its Broadway run, *A Chorus Line* was the longest running show in Broadway history, running for 6,137 performances, until it was surpassed by the Andrew Lloyd Weber juggernaut, *Cats*.

 Did you know that the original actor who played Zach was Robert LuPone? If you recognize that last name, then it makes sense that you bought this book. That's Patti's brother.

Bundts on this Island

Mango Bundt Cake with
Waiting-for-Lime-to-Begin Glaze

● ● ●

Inspired by ONCE ON THIS ISLAND

Music by Stephen Flaherty, *Book and Lyrics by* Lynn Ahrens

Opened on Broadway in 1990 at the Booth Theatre

ASAKA, BAKE ME A BUNDT CAKE! BASED ON ROSA GUY'S 1985 novel, *My Love, My Love; or, The Peasant Girl*, *Once on This Island* is a Caribbean retelling of Hans Christian Anderson's *The Little Mermaid*. Ti Moune, a young Antillean peasant girl, falls in love with Daniel, a rich nobleman, from the other side of the island. Unfortunately for Ti Moune, Daniel marries somebody else, and even more unfortunately, because of a pact she made with the gods to save his life, she is sentenced to death. Bummer, we know, but don't worry, the gods decide to turn her into a tree instead (hooray!). Speaking of trees, a signature of this Caribbean-inspired dish is its juicy mangoes. The gods would be so proud! Chock full of nuts, raisins, orange zest, lime juice, and sour cream, this Bundt cake *will* provide. There's a bit of booze in it, so if making it for one small girl, maybe leave it out. Either way, don't wait for life to begin: Go make this now.

RECIPE CONTINUES

FOR THE CAKE

2 sticks unsalted butter at room temperature, plus more for greasing the pan

2 cups all-purpose flour

1 teaspoon salt

½ teaspoon baking soda

2 teaspoons baking powder

2 teaspoons ground cinnamon

1 teaspoon freshly ground nutmeg

1 teaspoon ground allspice

1 cup light brown sugar

1 cup granulated sugar

4 large eggs, room temperature

1 cup sour cream

3 tablespoons dark rum

1 tablespoon vanilla extract

2 cups diced fresh mango (from 1 large or 2 small mangos)

1 cup chopped toasted walnuts or pecans

½ cup golden raisins

1 tablespoon orange zest (from 1 orange)

2 teaspoons lime zest (from 2 limes)

FOR THE GLAZE

2 cups confectioners' sugar

3 tablespoons freshly squeezed lime juice

1. Preheat the oven to 325°F.

2. Generously butter a large 9-inch Bundt pan with softened butter. (The more you grease it, the easier it'll be to get out. And softened butter works better than cooking spray here, so no cheating.)

3. In a large bowl, sift together the flour, salt, baking soda, baking powder, cinnamon, nutmeg, and allspice.

4. In the bowl of a stand mixer, cream together the butter and both sugars until light and fluffy, about 5 minutes. Add the eggs, one at a time, mixing thoroughly after each addition. Add the sour cream, rum, and vanilla and quickly mix in. Add the flour mixture and mix on low speed just until the flour disappears in the mix.

5. With a rubber spatula, fold in the 2 cups of mango, chopped toasted nuts, raisins, orange zest, and lime zest.

6. Pour the batter into the prepared Bundt pan and bake until a toothpick inserted comes out dry, approximately 1 hour and 10 minutes.

7. Allow to cool in the pan for 20 minutes, then run a small paring knife along the sides to ensure it'll flip out. Flip it out onto a cooling rack and allow to cool completely before glazing.

8. To make the glaze, whisk together the confectioners' sugar and lime juice until it's very thick but pourable. Pour all over the cake, allowing to drip down the sides. Allow the glaze to set, then serve.

COOKING NOTES

 You can add a nip of rum to your glaze, too. Just swap out 1 tablespoon of lime juice for light rum when you make it, or 2 tablespoons if the gods aren't watching.

 Be sure to be generous with the softened butter when coating the Bundt pan, or your story of being unable to get the cake out of the pan will be sadder than Ti Moune's.

LISTENING NOTES

 Did you know that Michael Arden's Tony-Award winning 2017 revival of *Once on This Island* was performed entirely on sand and had a live goat? Mmm, goat.

 The original production of *Once on This Island* put the fabulous LaChanze on the map. LaChanze's daughter, Celia Rose Gooding, is also an actress who was nominated for a Tony Award for *Jagged Little Pill*. Get us those genes! Actually, after making all these recipes, I don't know if we'll fit . . .

 In 2009, there was a production of *Once on This Island* at Berkeley Playhouse that cast a young unknown as Little Ti Moune. Her name was Zendaya.

Phantom of the Opera Cakes

Almond-Ask-of-You Cupcakes with Chocolate Ganache Frosting

• • •

Inspired by PHANTOM OF THE OPERA

Music by Andrew Lloyd Webber, *Lyrics by* Charles Hart, *Additional Lyrics by* Richard Stilgoe, *Book by* Richard Stilgoe *and* Andrew Lloyd Webber

Opened on Broadway in 1988 at the Majestic Theatre

THINK OF CUPCAKES, THINK OF CUPCAKES FONDLY, WHEN WE say goodbye! Based on Gaston Leroux's 1910 French novel of the same name, *Phantom of the Opera* centers around a disfigured masked man, who lives in the labyrinthine sewers beneath the Paris Opéra House, is deeply obsessed with opera, and becomes even more deeply obsessed with soprano Christine Daaé. The phantom wreaks havoc upon the denizens of the opera house when he doesn't get Christine or his way, which in turn teaches us the life lesson that you should never mess with an opera queen, especially when chandeliers are involved. One thing that might've placated the phantom: these cupcakes. A riff on opera cake, which normally involves a coffee-soaked almond cake with buttercream and chocolate glaze, this recipe simplifies things a bit. Almond cocoa cupcakes masquerade as opera cake and a whipped chocolate ganache frosting with instant espresso powder brings in the coffee flavor. Once you finish them, you'll be wishing they were somehow here again.

FOR THE CUPCAKES

¾ cup almond flour

¾ cups all-purpose flour

1 tablespoon cocoa
powder

1½ teaspoons baking
powder

½ teaspoon kosher salt

1 teaspoon vanilla extract

½ teaspoon almond
extract

½ cup buttermilk

1 stick (½ cup) butter, at
room temperature

1 cup granulated sugar

2 large eggs, room
temperature

**FOR THE WHIPPED
CHOCOLATE GANACHE
ICING**

8 ounces bittersweet
chocolate, finely
chopped

1 teaspoon espresso
powder

½ teaspoon kosher salt

1 cup heavy cream

TO MAKE THE CUPCAKES

1. Preheat the oven to 350°F. Line a 12-cup muffin tin with cupcake holders and spray
   everything with cooking spray.

2. In a large bowl, whisk together the almond flour, all-purpose flour, cocoa powder,
   baking powder, and salt. In a measuring glass, mix the vanilla extract, almond
   extract, and buttermilk together.

RECIPE CONTINUES

3. In the bowl of a stand mixer, cream the butter and sugar until light and fluffy. Add the eggs one at a time until fully incorporated. On low speed, add one-third flour mixture, half of the buttermilk mixture, another one-third of the flour mixture, the remaining buttermilk mixture, and finish with the final third of the flour.

4. Using a ¼-cup ice cream scoop, scoop the cupcake batter into the cupcake tins, dividing everything evenly, so that the batter comes up three-quarters of the way.

5. Bake for 20 to 25 minutes, until the cupcakes are lightly golden on top and a toothpick inserted into one comes out clean. Carefully lift the cupcakes out of the pan with an offset spatula and allow to cool on a wire rack before icing.

TO MAKE THE FROSTING

1. Place the chopped chocolate, espresso powder, and salt in the bowl of a stand mixer. Heat the cream in a small pan or pot until just bubbling around the edges, then pour over the chocolate. Allow the warm cream to melt the chocolate for 3 minutes without stirring.

2. Stir with a rubber spatula until all the chocolate is melted. (If it all doesn't melt, it's okay. Place the bowl of the stand mixer on top of a pot of simmering water without letting the bottom touch the water. Keep stirring until all the chocolate is melted.) Now set the melted chocolate aside and let sit for 1 hour or until it reaches room temperature.

3. When the chocolate is at room temperature, attach the whisk attachment to your mixer and mix on medium-high speed for 3 minutes, or until the frosting is light and fluffy. (If the ganache won't fluff up, refrigerate it for 5 to 10 minutes and try again.)

4. Use an offset spatula or piping bag to frost your cupcakes. They'll keep in a covered container for up to 3 days in the refrigerator.

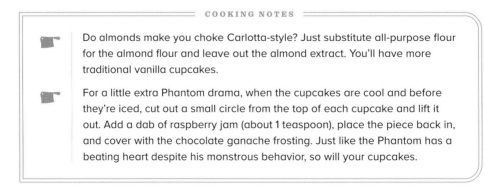

=== COOKING NOTES ===

Do almonds make you choke Carlotta-style? Just substitute all-purpose flour for the almond flour and leave out the almond extract. You'll have more traditional vanilla cupcakes.

For a little extra Phantom drama, when the cupcakes are cool and before they're iced, cut out a small circle from the top of each cupcake and lift it out. Add a dab of raspberry jam (about 1 teaspoon), place the piece back in, and cover with the chocolate ganache frosting. Just like the Phantom has a beating heart despite his monstrous behavior, so will your cupcakes.

At the time of *Swiss Chards*' publication, *The Phantom of the Opera* is currently the longest running show in Broadway history, having stayed open since its premiere in 1988. It has grossed over $6 billion worldwide.

 Roger Waters, former Pink Floyd vocalist and bassist, claims that the main ascending and descending chord progression from the titular song, "Phantom of the Opera," was plagiarized from the bass line in Pink Floyd's "Echoes." He never took legal action. Why? Because, as he puts it, "Life's too long to bother with suing Andrew F****ing Lloyd Webber."

 The show is known for its foggy atmosphere, which is created nightly with the use of 400 pounds of dry ice! Guess that explains the Phantom's chilly demeanor.

My Fair Ladyfingers

Do-little Berry Tiramisu

• • •

Inspired by MY FAIR LADY

Music by Frederick Loewe, *Lyrics and Book by* Alan Jay Lerner

Opened on Broadway in 1956 at the Mark Hellinger Theatre

COULD HAVE EATEN LADYFINGERS ALL NIGHT, LADYFINGERS ALL night, and could still have eaten some more! Based on George Bernard Shaw's 1913 play, *Pygmalion*, *My Fair Lady* follows Cockney flower girl, Eliza Doolittle (no relation to the doctor), who becomes the mission of a phonetician (take note of the rhyme, Lerner), Henry Higgins, to be transformed, with elocution lessons, into a proper lady. This musical comes from a long line of cisgender white men who feel it is important to change a woman, and it's been revived on Broadway at least four times! You know what else is constantly revived? Tiramisu. But we promise you haven't been accustomed to this one. With lots of berries and elderflower liqueur, in honor of our flower lady, and bourbon, in honor of our phonetician, this bright, tart tiramisu is loverly indeed, especially with dehydrated raspberry powder sifted all over the top. It takes no time to put together and the best part is, you make it ahead . . . so you don't have to do anything the day you serve it. Just you wait: You're going to love it.

2 cups blackberries
2 cups raspberries
½ cup granulated sugar
Zest of 1 lemon
1 tablespoon lemon juice

3 tablespoons elderflower liqueur
16 ounces mascarpone, softened (left out of the fridge for 30 minutes)

2 tablespoons bourbon
1 teaspoon vanilla extract
1 cup heavy cream
24 ladyfingers
1 cup freeze-dried raspberries

1. In a ceramic bowl, combine the blackberries, raspberries, ¼ cup sugar, lemon zest, lemon juice, and elderflower liqueur. Mash up some of the berries as you stir to release their juices, then allow to sit, covered with plastic wrap, for 2 hours.

2. In a large bowl, whisk together the mascarpone, ¼ cup sugar, bourbon, and vanilla. In a separate bowl or mixer, whisk the heavy cream until soft peaks form, about 1 minute. Fold the heavy cream into the mascarpone mixture.

3. In an 8-by-8-inch baking dish, layer in half of the ladyfingers (you may need to break a few to make them fit in one layer). Top with half of the berry mixture, then spread on half of the mascarpone. Top with the remaining ladyfingers, the remaining berry mixture, and finish with the rest of the mascarpone. Cover with plastic wrap and refrigerate for at least 4 hours, but preferably overnight.

4. Right before serving, place the freeze-dried raspberries in a freezer bag and smash with a rolling pin to make a bright red powder. Pour into a sifter and sift over the top of the tiramisu before serving.

RECIPE CONTINUES

This tiramisu can still make you gavotte without the booze. Try adding a tablespoon of pomegranate juice to the berries instead of the elderflower liqueur. And in the mascarpone layer, skip the bourbon and double the vanilla.

 The elements of this tiramisu are all flexible: Don't like elderflower liqueur? Try maraschino liqueur. Don't like blackberries? Try strawberries. Just as long as you have something to dip your ladyfingers into, and some kind of flavoring for the mascarpone that goes on top, you'll be dancing all night indeed.

 The show's original title was *Liza*, which then gave way to *Lady Liza*, but Rex Harrison, the original Higgins (in very Higgins style) didn't like that it broadcast that his character was only a secondary character and aggressively campaigned for a new title.

 Almost all of Audrey Hepburn's singing in the film adaptation was dubbed by Marni Nixon, who also famously dubbed the singing roles of Ana in *The King and I* and Maria in *West Side Story*.

 "The Rain in Spain" is one of *My Fair Lady*'s most cherished numbers, but it's actually factually (another great rhyme, Lerner) inaccurate. Spain's northern hills and mountains get far more rainfall yearly than its plains in the south. Tsk, tsk, Lerner and Loewe!

Joseph and the Amazing Technicolor Cream Float

Scarlet and Black and Ochre and Peach Ice Cream Sodas

• • •

Inspired by JOSEPH AND THE AMAZING TECHNICOLOR DREAMCOAT

Music by Andrew Lloyd Webber, *Lyrics by* Tim Rice

Opened on Broadway in 1982 at the Royale Theatre

AND IN THE KITCHEN, ICE CREAM WAS MELTING, SELTZER WAS seltzing, any float will do. Based on that good ole' Old Testament story of Joseph, *Joseph and the Amazing Technicolor Dreamcoat* is a cautionary tale about favoritism and the trials and tribulations of being profiled for wearing rainbow-colored coats. Poor Joseph gets sold by his jealous brothers as a slave, is lusted after by Mrs. Potiphar, and is consequently thrown in prison. He then ascends to the Pharaoh's good graces as his interpreter of dreams and is ultimately reunited with his hungry brothers whom he graciously forgives and shoves out of the way for one final solo number. You won't be flying solo with this ice cream soda, however, which will have you living your youth again. It's as easy as this: Make a simple vanilla bean syrup (vanilla beans are pricey, so you may need to borrow from your Pharaoh daddy) and pour it over some colorful scoops of raspberry, peach, or mango sorbet, then top with soda. We're going for dreamcoat colors here, so pick any flavors that have scarlet or black or ochre or peach or ruby or olive or violet or fawn or lilac or gold or chocolate or mauve . . .

RECIPE CONTINUES

FOR THE VANILLA BEAN SYRUP

1 cup granulated sugar
1 cup water
1 vanilla bean

FOR THE FLOAT

1 quart French vanilla ice cream
1 quart raspberry sorbet

1 quart peach or mango sorbet
1 liter bottle soda water

1. First, make the vanilla bean syrup. In a saucepan, bring the sugar and water to a boil and cook until the sugar dissolves. Turn off the heat and, with a paring knife, slice the vanilla bean down the middle lengthwise. Using the side of the knife, scrape the bean on both sides to pick up all the seeds. Place into the saucepan, along with the remaining vanilla bean, and allow to steep for 30 minutes. Remove the bean and refrigerate the syrup until ready to use. (It will keep for 1 week in the fridge.)

2. To make your 'cream floats, in large glasses put in 1 scoop of the French vanilla ice cream, 1 scoop of the raspberry sorbet, and 1 scoop of the peach or mango sorbet. Add a tablespoon of the vanilla bean syrup to each glass in front of your guests (so everyone can see the colors as they all blend together), slowly pour in the soda water, stirring as you do, so the flavors meld together. Fill up the glass (at least ½ cup of soda water per glass) and serve with straws.

If you're more of a chocolate person, we won't close the door on you. Skip the vanilla bean syrup and the peach/mango sorbet, double up the raspberry and add a tablespoon of your favorite chocolate syrup instead. You'll have a chocolate raspberry 'cream float . . . a dream come true.

 For the Mrs. Potiphar in your life, skip the vanilla ice cream, use just mango and peach sorbets, and add a splash of Amaro to the mix before stirring in the soda water. You'll be calypso-ing in no time.

LISTENING NOTES

 In 1968, *Joseph* . . . was first presented as a 15-minute pop cantata at a preparatory school in London. The 1999 film adaptation nods to its preparatory origins as the show takes place in a school auditorium.

 Twelve years into its 1979 run, the original tour of *Joseph* . . . broke the Guinness Book of Records for longest tour.

 One author of this book directed a production of *Joseph* . . . in college and he infamously purports to have done a minimalist rendering of the musical and used just two blocks for a throne. And look where that landed him—right in this book.

Acknowledgments

Alison Fargis, who immediately sparked to this idea, helped us find it a perfect home, and fielded our various questions throughout the process.

Diana Fithian, our earliest champion, who helped us fine-tune the recipes for the proposal.

Ann Treistman, an incredible editor and champion, who graciously let us be as obscure as we wanted about musicals and never stepped on our puns and recipes, no matter how corny (sorry we had to); Allison Chi, Devon Zahn, Jess Murphy, and Rhina Garcia, who worked tirelessly to bring this book to fruition and to the world. Our full cast of recipe testers, who generously volunteered over Instagram. The outpouring was unbelievable—we had two testers for every recipe—and the food in this book would *not* be as good without you. Time for your curtain call: Amanda Agosti, Charlotte Austin, Julie Banks, Hannah Barr-DiChiara, Monica Bartz-Gallagher, Helen Bi, Amanda Birkhead, Samy Burch, Jan Byrer, Nina Camic, Katie Carter, Mariel Childress, Gregory Corning, Maria Crawford, Peter Dennehy, Oscar Denton, Denise Dunn, Basak Efe, Zahra Elkhafaifi, Felicia Fasano, Ben Fishner, Lindsey Fox, Sara Futch, Susan P. Garzon, Angeline Gaw, Sarah Gorglione, Josh Gunter, Devon Harlos, Gretchen Hermann, Chloe Hillmer, Michael Hundgen, Jennifer Jackson, Judy Jackson, Sade Jimoh, Marcus Kaye, John Kazlauskas, Erin Kelley, Mary Ann Kiczek, Alyssa King, Judson Kniffen, Mireille Labrie, Matt Lardie, Carrol Lee, Evonne Leeper, Abigail Mayeda, Walter Mayes, Kenny Mellman, Priscilla Midani, Dani Miller, Michael Moore, Colleen Moran, Lena Moy-Borgen, Lori Nelson, Sunni Newton, Kelly Novitski, Becky Nuse, Jean O'Donnell, Kyle O'Donnell, Lara Paquette, Steve Parkinson, Andrea Passafiume, Doris Peterson, Laura Riggs, Terri Robinson, Audrey Rufe, Chelsea J. Samuel, Kay Sanders, Katya Schapiro, Ron Sharon-Zipser, Catherine Sheridan, Michael Sherman, Loren Shlaes, Abigail Skinner, Derek Smith, Felicity Spector, Sarah Stokes, Deirdre Synan, Brigham Taylor, Tony Thaweethai, Dory Trimble, and Thomas Yi.

We're deeply grateful to our friends and family who weighed in on our puns and buns: Toby Brooks, Leah Burnie, Tim Federle, Jonathan Glick, Mollie Glick, Sas Goldberg, Kevin Lin, Ilyana Maisonet, Cristin Milioti, Ana Nogueira, Augustus Prew, Zachary Prince, Ben Rimalower, Charles Rogers, Jeffery Self, Alysha Umphress, Brandon Uranowitz, and Jake Wilson.

And, finally, Justin "Squigs" Robertson, who signed on to this wacky project blindly and with love. Your illustrations make this book sing.

Index

About the Authors

GIDEON GLICK was nominated for the 2019 Tony Award for Best Supporting Actor in Broadway's *To Kill a Mockingbird*, written by Academy Award–winner Aaron Sorkin and based on Harper Lee's Pulitzer Prize–winning novel.

Since making his Broadway debut as Ernst in the original cast of the groundbreaking musical *Spring Awakening*, Glick has been seen on Broadway in Joshua Harmon's *Significant Other*, for which he earned a 2017 Drama League Award nomination for Distinguished Performance, and Julie Taymor's production of *Spider-Man: Turn Off the Dark*. Off-Broadway, he has starred in the critically acclaimed production of *Little Shop of Horrors,* in MacArthur Fellow and Obie-winner Samuel Hunter's *The Harvest* and *The Few*, Tony-winner and Pulitzer-finalist Stephen Karam's *Speech and Debate*, Broadway god Stephen Sondheim's *Into the Woods*, and many more.

On the big screen, Gideon can be seen in Scott Cooper's *The Pale Blue Eye,* Noah Baumbach's *White Noise* and *Marriage Story,* Gary Ross' *Ocean's 8,* the film adaptation of *Speech & Debate*, *Fit Model, Song One, A Case of You*, *Gods Behaving Badly*, and *One Last Thing . . . .* On television, Glick can be seen as Alfie in Amazon's hit show *The Marvelous Mrs. Maisel* and as Jess in HBO Max's *The Other Two*. He previously appeared in TBS's *The Detour*, FX's *Man Seeking Woman*, Lifetime's *Devious Maids*, and in CBS's *Elementary* and *The Good Wife*.

You can keep up with Gideon on Twitter or Instagram by following @gidglick. He currently resides in New York City with his husband and dog.

ADAM ROBERTS is a self-taught cook and humor writer whose food blog, *The Amateur Gourmet*, was named "the eleventh best food blog of all time" by *First We Feast*. He is the author of two books, *The Amateur Gourmet* (Bantam Dell, 2005) and *Secrets of the Best Chefs* (Artisan, 2013), which was named The Best Cookbook of the Year by *The Daily Meal.*

Roberts has written articles and recipes for such outlets as the *Washington Post*, *Los Angeles Times, Food & Wine, Salon, Serious Eats*, and *Food52*. He was the host of the Food Network's first-ever web series, *The FN Dish*, and a staff writer and then story editor on the ABC sitcom, *The Real O'Neals*.

His podcast, *The Amateur Gourmet Podcast*, features intimate interviews with food-world stars like Ruth Reichl, Fergus Henderson, and Melissa Clark. You can follow his cooking adventures on Instagram @amateurgourmet, read his weekly recipe updates in *The Amateur Gourmet Newsletter* on Substack, and watch his *Amateur Gourmet Show* on YouTube. He currently lives in Los Angeles with his husband and dog, just like Gideon.

JUSTIN "SQUIGS" ROBERTSON has become one of Broadway theatre's most acclaimed caricaturists in the past decade, hailed by the *New York Times* as one of the "Line King's Heirs," carrying on the traditions exemplified by legendary *Times* artist Al Hirschfeld. He is the co-creator, illustrator, and designer of The Lights of Broadway Show Cards™ trading cards; and his illustrations have been seen regularly since 2010 as the Broadway Ink feature on leading Broadway news site Broadway.com. His work has also appeared in the *New York Times, Wall Street Journal, Los Angeles Times, Variety*, and in promotional campaigns for Actors' Equity, Broadway Cares/Equity Fights AIDS, the Theatre World Awards, and theatrical productions in New York, London, and around the world.

As an actor and vocalist, he has been seen on the stages of regional theaters and theme parks across the country. He was born and raised in Oregon, lived in Los Angeles for many years, and now calls New York City his home.

You can follow more of Justin's work on Twitter and Instagram at @squigsrobertson. He doesn't have a dog but might be reconsidering this situation.